Exquisite Modular Origami II

Cover Menu

Exquisite Modular Origami II
Meenakshi Mukerji

Compound of 5 Tetrahedra · Ornamental Cube · Ornamental Omega 5 · Curled Sonobe · Columbine · Curly Locks · Gerbera · Fanfare · Origami My Heart · Poinsettia 2 · Zinnia 2 · Flora · Centaury · Crape Jasmine · Frangipani · Cupidon · Decorative Cube · Hearty Cube · Big Dot Cube · Dogwood Cube · Patterned Skeletohedron 3 · Juhi Sonobe

It seems like there are myriad modular origami designs out there these days; anything that joins goes. However, in this book, Meenakshi Mukerji's sixth, she still has much more to offer, with the designs presented some of her best yet. After a very successful *Exquisite Modular Origami*, this second volume is a natural follow up. Handpicked by the author, the models are not only beautiful, but have been subjected to rigorous design criteria such as sturdiness of the locking mechanism, easy starting paper proportions, mostly squares, absence of inserts and separate joining units, and appealing aesthetics of the finished art.

The designs are all-new and like before, works of three new, very creative guest artists have been included as well. In grayscale, the book is practically a bargain because it is as effective as folding from a color book. Color photos of most designs are on the cover for your viewing pleasure. Just when you think you are running out of satisfying modular origami to fold, here now you have dozens more exciting new ones to enjoy. Do visit the author's popular website www.origamee.net for more ideas and color photos.

Exquisite Modular Origami II

Meenakshi Mukerji

Copyright © 2015 by Meenakshi Mukerji - all rights reserved worldwide. No part of this book may be reproduced or transmitted in any form or by any means, electronic or mechanical, including photocopying, recording, or by any information storage or retrieval system without written permission from the author. The designs in this book are intended for personal use only. Any commercial use requires consent from the author. Contact information may be found in www.origamee.net.

Frangipani © Natalia Romanenko
Cupidon © Uniya Filonova
Crape Jasmine © Narong Krined

ISBN-13: 978-1517500948
ISBN-10: 151750094X

(This is a second volume of *Exquisite Modular Origami*, 2011, ISBN 978-1463707606.)

Overleaf: Fanfare showing the Corona Harmony paper it is folded from.

Hydrangea Cube (page 69)

To all origami lovers

Acknowledgement

I would like to start by thanking those who directly contributed to the book. Thanks to Natalia Romanenko of Moldova for her beautiful Frangipani (page 76), Uniya Filonova of Russia for her lovely Cupidon (page 78), and Narong Krined of Thailand for his wonderful Crape Jasmine (page 80), and the respective design photos on the back cover, second row.

For diagram testing, I would like to thank Rui Roda of Portugal and Charul Patil of India who tested extensively for me. They always got back with meaningful feedback faster than I could imagine or expect. They even posted enticing photos of the tests on social media which helped spread the word about the book well before its release. Also, thanks to Rui for the Heart Petals folding and photographs (page 58), and to Charul for the Flora folding and photograph (page 22).

Thanks to Kedar Amladi of California for patiently taking the following amazing photographs with his innovative homemade light box: Zinnia 2 (back cover, top row), Ornamental Omega 5 and Ornamental Cube (cover, top row), Curly Locks and Curled Sonobe (cover, middle row), and Hydrangea Cube (page iv). Thanks to Ekaterina Lukasheva of California for some photo editing help.

Thanks to J C Nolan of California, for writing an insightful and kind Foreword for this book. He also patiently helped me with digital processing of a cover image.

Artists whose works have influenced some of my designs have been acknowledged alongside the respective diagrams. Immense thanks to all of them for their extreme generosity in granting me permission to publish works derived from their original ideas.

Thanks to all those who constantly encourage me to come up with new designs and write more books. I wish to thank the visitors of my website, www.origamee.net and also the visitors of facebook.com/origamee.net, for their continued support and enthusiasm. Huge thanks to all in my family as well as my friends here in the US, in India, and around the world for providing me with endless inspiration.

A final note of thanks goes to Klaus Peters who sadly passed away last year. My debut in the published world is due to his belief in my work and his kindness. The science and technology publications community, and also the recreational mathematics publications community miss him dearly.

Contents

Acknowledgement vi
Picture Index viii
Foreword xi
Preface xii
Introduction 1
Origami Tips, Tools and Paper 2
Origami Basics 4
Platonic, Archimedean and Kepler-Poinsot Solids 8
Hearty Cube and Variations 10
Decorative Cube and Variations 13
Patterned Skeloctahedron and Variations 18
Flora 23
Curly Locks 26
Zinnia 2 and Variation 29
Curled Sonobe 33
Juhi Sonobe 35
Centaury 37
Columbine 39
Gerbera and Variations 42
Poinsettia Floral Ball 2 45
Fanfare and Variation 49
Origami My Heart 52
Heart Petals 56
Ornamental Omega 5 59
Compound of Five Tetrahedra 63
Ornamental Cube 66
Dogwood Cube and Flower 70
Big Dot Cube 74
Frangipani 76
Cupidon 78
Crape Jasmine 80
Bibliography and Suggested Reading 82
Suggested Websites 85
About Author and Guest Contributors 86

Picture Index

This index includes paper recommendations and sizes along with finished sizes and difficulty levels of a design. Not all variations are shown. Difficulty level key - **S**: Simple, **I**: Intermediate, **HI**: High Intermediate, **A**: Advance.

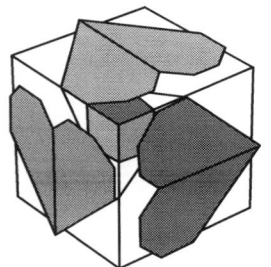

**Hearty Cube
Page 10**
3"x6" rectangles of two sided paper,
6 sheets.
Finished height 2".
(S)

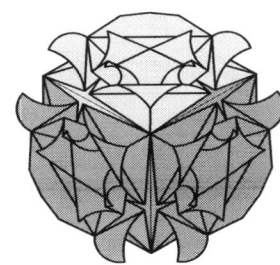

**Decorative Cube
Page 13**
6" squares of Corona Harmony or other paper,
6 sheets.
Finished height ~3.5"
(S)

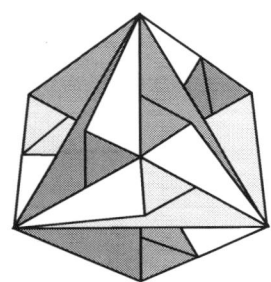

**Patterned Skeloctahedron 1
Page 18**
4" squares of 2 sided paper,
6 sheets.
Finished height ~2.8"
(S)

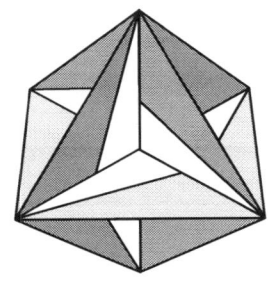

**Patterned Skeloctahedron 2
Page 20**
4" squares of 2 sided paper,
6 sheets.
Finished height ~2.8"
(S)

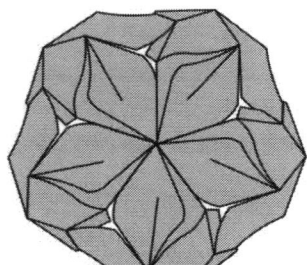

**Flora
Page 23**
3" squares of any paper, 30 sheets.
Finished height ~4"
(I)

**Curly Locks
Page 26**
4" squares of any paper, 30 sheets.
Finished height ~4.5"
(I)

**Zinnia 2
Page 29**
4"x6" rectangles of any paper,
30 sheets.
Finished height ~5.5"
(A)

**Zinnia 2 Variation
Page 32**
4"x6" rectangles of kami,
30 sheets.
Finished height ~5.5"
(A)

Exquisite Modular Origami II

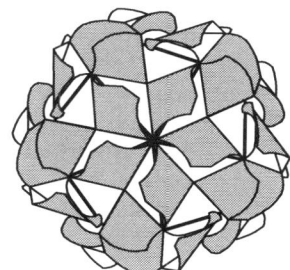

Curled Sonobe
Page 33
4" squares of two sided paper,
30 sheets.
Finished height ~5"
(I)

Juhi Sonobe
Page 35
4" squares of two sided paper,
30 sheets.
Finished height ~5"
(I)

Centaury
Page 37
3"x5.5" rectangles of any paper,
30 sheets.
Finished height ~6"
(I)

Columbine
Page 39
3"x5.5" rectangles of two sided paper,
30 sheets.
Finished height ~6"
(I)

Gerbera
Page 42
3"x5.5" rectangles of two sided paper,
30 sheets.
Finished height ~6"
(HI)

Poinsettia 2
Page 45
2"x4" rectangles of two sided paper,
30 sheets.
Finished height ~5.5"
(HI)

Fanfare
Page 49
3"x6" rectangles of kami,
30 sheets.
Finished height ~5"
(HI)

Fanfare Variation
Page 51
3"x9" rectangles of two sided paper, 30 sheets.
Finished height ~5"
(HI)

Origami My Heart
Page 52
4" squares of kami,
30 sheets.
Finished height ~4.2"
(A)

Heart Petals
Page 56
2.67"x4" rectangles of printer paper,
30 sheets.
Finished height ~4.2"
(A)

**Ornamental Omega 5
Page 59**
6" squares of any paper cut into pentagons, 12 sheets.
Finished height ~5.5"
(A)

**Compound of 5 Tetrahedra
Page 63**
4" squares of printer paper,
60 sheets.
Finished height ~6.5"
(A)

**Ornamental Cube
Page 66**
8" squares of any paper, 6 sheets.
Finished height ~2.8"
(A)

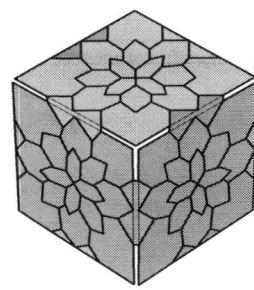

**Hydrangea Cube
Page 69**
8" squares of any paper, 6 sheets.
Finished height ~2.8"
(A)

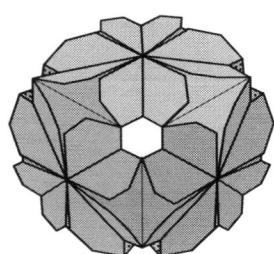

**Dogwood Cube
Page 70**
6" squares of Corona Harmony paper, 6 sheets.
Finished height ~2.12"
(A)

**Dogwood Flower and Leaves
Page 73**
6" square of Corona Harmony paper.
Finished size 3"
(A)

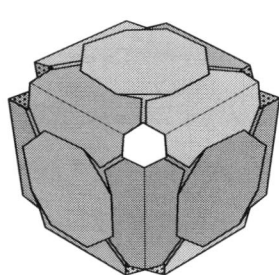

**Big Dot Cube
Page 74**
6" squares of Corona Harmony paper, 6 sheets.
Finished height ~2.12"
(A)

**Frangipani
Page 76**
2"x4" rectangles of two sided paper, 30 sheets.
Finished height ~4"
(HI)

**Cupidon
Page 78**
3" squares of two sided paper,
30 sheets.
Finished height ~4.8"
(HI)

**Crape Jasmine
Page 80**
4" squares of two sided paper,
30 sheets.
Finished height ~4"
(HI)

Exquisite Modular Origami II

Foreword

I first made the acquaintance of Meenakshi Mukerji in early 2010 when I was working at a large Silicon Valley tech firm and got into a philosophical debate with a fellow origami fan whether the large multi-unit origami assembly on my colleague's desk was actually a yet-undiscovered polyhedron (as she claimed) or just another variation of one already known. I immediately got on-line to research the problem, and found the answer in a lovely, well-illustrated article which clearly laid out the possibilities and variations to be achieved with modular origami.

As it turns out, that article was written by Mukerji who several months later gently coaxed me back into the origami community after a twenty year absence when: she invited me to a local folders meeting; presented me with a signed copy of her newest book (which included a modular base on a variation of one of my earlier works); and challenged me to finding a solution to a new puzzle in the form of creating a simple assembly sequence for Mancini's SIP.

Over the years I've had the pleasure of getting to know Mukerji well and the one thing that resonates the most for me is her passion for sharing. Having created her first book almost entirely in isolation and being one of the original awardees of the OrigamiUSA "Florence Temko" award for making a meaningful contribution to the origami community, for Mukerji that spirit of engagement and expanding community shines brighter and brighter as her catalog of amazing creations expands and her mastery and creativity expand right along-side.

With "Exquisite Modular Origami II" she continues to follow this path building both on her skill as a designer and as engineer this newest collection celebrates an exploration of more elaborate shadings and nuance that the folder can bring to the process. As always, her work is lovely and engaging and with this work Mukerji's explorations expand from simple step-by-step instructions to creating a new realm where each model itself becomes a jumping point for further exploration.

— **JC Nolan**, Chair of the OrigamiUSA Archives committee and author of 5 books including *"Creating Origami: An Exploration into the Process of Designing Paper Sculpture"*

Preface

After a wonderfully warm reception of the first *Exquisite Modular Origami*, it is my pleasure to present a second volume as a natural follow up. I continue to make this book in grayscale because it keeps it inexpensive, making it accessible to a wider audience. The end result is the same whether you fold from a color book or a grayscale one. Color photographs of majority of the designs are on the cover for your referencing convenience and viewing pleasure. Additional color photos are on my website origamee.net, and also on facebook.com/origamee.net.

It seems that there are myriad modular designs out there these days. Anything that joins can pass as modular origami. But I have subjected my designs to some rigorous self-imposed criteria before handpicking them for the book. First of all, of course, they have to be aesthetically pleasing with clean well-defined lines. Second, they must be sturdy and should be able to withstand a moderate amount of handling without falling apart. Third, the starting papers must be squares and, if not, then the starting proportions should be easily obtainable. Lastly, the models should not rely on inserts or separate joining tabs.

The designs presented in this book are mostly new and previously unpublished, though some may have appeared in origami journals. Unlike some other books which have a considerable amount of repeated material, I try to keep the book at least ninety percent new. The book has been a labor of love. I have single handedly dealt with everything from diagramming my designs to most of the photography, cover design, book layout, you name it – and, of course, I put keen attention to perfection.

The first few pages of the book contain origami basics and other material that must be included in any modular origami book in order for it to be complete. Also provided are handy polyhedron charts for referencing during model assembly. Folding tips, types of paper and other topics important to folding origami, particularly modular origami, have been discussed as well.

As in my other books, I have introduced designs of new and upcoming artists whose works call for more visibility than they already have. The artists have been introduced at the end (page 88). Their diagramming styles have been preserved and not changed merely for the sake of consistency across the book.

The diagrams in this book follow standard origami symbols. The language of origami diagramming is very powerful and can be attributed mostly to origami master Akira Yoshizawa. Although written descriptions are generally provided with the diagrams, they are mostly quite redundant barring certain special circumstances when the need may arise. To keep the diagrams simple and neat I have refrained from showing layers except when necessary.

The book is organized in a loose structure of easy to difficult with some exceptions. Overall, none of the designs are of complex level. The book is meant for audiences 12 years of age or older who are looking to go beyond the traditional cranes and frogs. Although not aimed at beginners, gifted beginners can certainly tackle the designs presented in this book. Sometimes the units or modules separately may seem quite mundane, but the assembled finished model is always like a pleasant surprise waiting to be cherished at the end. I hope you find hours of enjoyment and relaxation and are tempted to design your own origami, after having folded from this book.

— Cupertino, CA, October 2015

Introduction

The word origami is based on two Japanese words: *oru* (to fold) and *kami* (paper). Although this ancient art of paper folding started in Japan and China, origami is now a household word around the world. Most people have probably folded at least a paper boat or an airplane. Origami has evolved immensely in the present times and is much more than a handful of traditional models. Modular origami, origami sculptures, and origami tessellations are but some of the newer forms of the art. The method of designing models has also evolved. While some models are designed the old fashioned way using mostly imagination and some trial and error, others are designed with complex mathematical algorithms using the computer.

Modular origami, as the name implies, involves assembling several, usually identical, modules or units to form one finished model. The beauty lies in folding relatively simple units leading to an aesthetic complex structure. While an understanding of mathematics is useful for designing, it is not crucial for merely following instructions to assemble. Even though mathematics may not be one's forte, one can still make modular origami and perhaps the process might impart a deeper appreciation for the mathematical principles involved. Like any multi-stepped task it requires patience, diligence and a bit of practice. It is always a pleasure to see the finished model at the end, the outcome is often greatly different than the individual parts would have initially suggested. Aesthetics and mathematics brilliantly come together in these wonderful structures to satisfy our many senses.

Modular origami can be fit relatively easily into one's busy schedule if one can be a bit organized. Unlike many other art forms, long uninterrupted stretches of time are not required. This makes it a perfect artistic endeavor given the hectic, fast paced life that we all lead. Upon mastering one unit which usually doesn't take long, several more can be folded anywhere anytime, including the short breaks between other chores. When the units are all folded, the final assembly can also be done slowly over time. Modular origami is great for folding during the inevitable waits at airports, doctor's offices or even on long flights. Just remember to carry your paper, diagrams and maybe a box for the finished units that are 3D. It is best to assemble the units at home because finished models are not easy to carry.

Assembly of the units that comprise a model may at first seem very puzzling to the novice, or even downright impossible. But understanding certain aspects can considerably simplify the process. First, one must determine whether a unit is a face unit, an edge unit, or a vertex unit, i.e., whether a unit identifies with a face, an edge or a vertex respectively, of a polyhedron. Face units are the easiest to identify. The vertex units are not as common, some examples being David Mitchell's Electra [Mit00] and Ravi Apte's Universal Vertex Modules [Tan02]. Most modular units tend to be edge units. For edge units there is a second step involved - one must identify which part of the unit, which is far from looking like an edge, actually maps to the edge of a polyhedron. Although it may appear perplexing at first, on closer look one may find that it is not an impossible task. Once the identifications are made and the folder can see through the maze of superficial designs and perceive the unit as a face, an edge, or a vertex, assembly becomes simple. It is then just a matter of following the structure of the underlying polyhedron to assemble the units and complete the model. With some relatively simple folding you can arrive at these amazingly beautiful complex structures.

Origami Tips, Tools and Paper

Origami Tips

- Use paper of the same thickness and texture for all units. This ensures that the look and strength of the finished models will be uniform. Virtually any paper from printer paper to gift-wrap may be used to fold origami.

- Make sure that the grain of the paper is oriented the same way for all your units. To determine the grain of the paper, gently bend paper both horizontally and vertically. The grain of the paper is said to lie along the direction that offers less resistance.

- Precision is particularly crucial in modular origami, so your folds need to be as accurate as possible. Only then will the finished models look symmetric, neat and appealing. Take your time to fold and do not rush.

- A well-lit area is highly recommended. Also, mountain folds are more easily visible, so try to make your reference creases mountain folds whenever possible.

- It is advisable to fold a trial unit before starting your project. In some cases the finished unit is much smaller than the starting paper, while in others it is not. Making a trial unit will give you an idea of what the size of the finished units, and hence a finished model might be, for a given paper size. It will also give you an idea of the paper properties and whether the paper you selected is suitable for the model you are making.

- After you have determined your paper size and type (discussed later), procure all the paper you need for the model before starting. If you do not have all the paper at the beginning, you may discover, as has been my experience, that you are not able to find more paper of the same kind to finish your model.

- If a step seems difficult, looking ahead to the next step often helps a great deal. This is because the execution of a current step results in what is diagrammed in the next step.

- Assembly aids such as miniature clothespins or paper clips are often advisable, especially for beginners. Some assemblies simply need them irrespective of your level. These pins or clips may be removed as the assembly progresses or at the end.

- During assembly, putting together the last few units, especially the very last one, can be challenging. During those times, remember that it is paper you are working with and not metal! Paper is flexible and can be bent or flexed for ease of assembly.

- After completion, hold the model in both hands and compress gently to make sure that all the tabs are securely and completely in their corresponding pockets. Finish by working your fingers around the ball.

- Use templates in unusual folding situations such as folding into thirds, to reduce unwanted creases. The templates in turn can be created using origami methods.

- Procure a minimal set of basic handy tools listed next. These tools assist in sizing paper, making neat and crisp creases, curling paper, accessing hard to reach areas, as well as assembling the units.

Origami Tools

- **Creasing Tools:** The most basic tool that is used in origami is a bone folder. It allows making precise and crisp creases and prevents your nails from being sore when folding excessively. Substitutes might be credit cards or other similar objects.

- **Cutting Tools:** Although cutting is prohibited in pure origami, cutting tools are required for the initial sizing of the paper. A great cutting tool would be a paper guillotine but it is bulky and may not be readily accessible to all people. I find a portable photo trimmer with replaceable blades to be a great substitute. They are inexpensive and easily carried anywhere. Scissors may be used but it is very difficult to get straight cuts.

- **Curling Tools:** Many origami models involve curling. Chop sticks, knitting needles, screwdrivers, or similar objects such as narrow pencils work well for curling paper.

- **Other Tools:** Miniature clothespins may be used during model assembly as temporary aids to hold two adjacent units together. The clothespins may be removed as the assembly progresses or after completion. Tweezers may be used to access hard to reach places or for folding paper that becomes too small to maneuver with fingers.

Origami Paper

Origami can be folded from practically any type of paper. But every model has a paper that works best for it and mostly experience can tell which one. Some models might require sturdy paper while some others might require paper that creases softly. Origami made from company logo paper make good gifts for colleagues while discarded sheet music can be used for folding gifts for music teachers. I have used recycled paper for folding without people even guessing. For finished models in which the reverse side of the paper is not visible, one can reuse paper that is printed on one side. Repurposing paper goes along the lines of being environmentally friendly, which is quite important in this day and age.

The following is a list of readily available origami paper.

- **Kami:** This is the most readily available origami paper. It is solidly colored on one side and white on the other.

- **Duo:** Paper that is one color on one side and a different color on the other.

- **Printer paper:** Paper, white or colored, that is commonly used in home or office computer printers.

- **Mono:** These papers have the same color on both sides. Printer paper is an example of mono paper.

- **Harmony paper:** Paper that has some harmonious pattern formed by various colors blending into one another. When used it can have a dramatic effect on some designs.

- **Chiyogami:** Origami paper with patterns, usually small, printed on it.

- **Washi:** Handmade Japanese paper with plant fiber in the pulp that gives it texture.

- **Foil backed paper:** These have metallic foil on one side and paper on the other side.

Origami Basics

This is a list of commonly used origami symbols and bases.

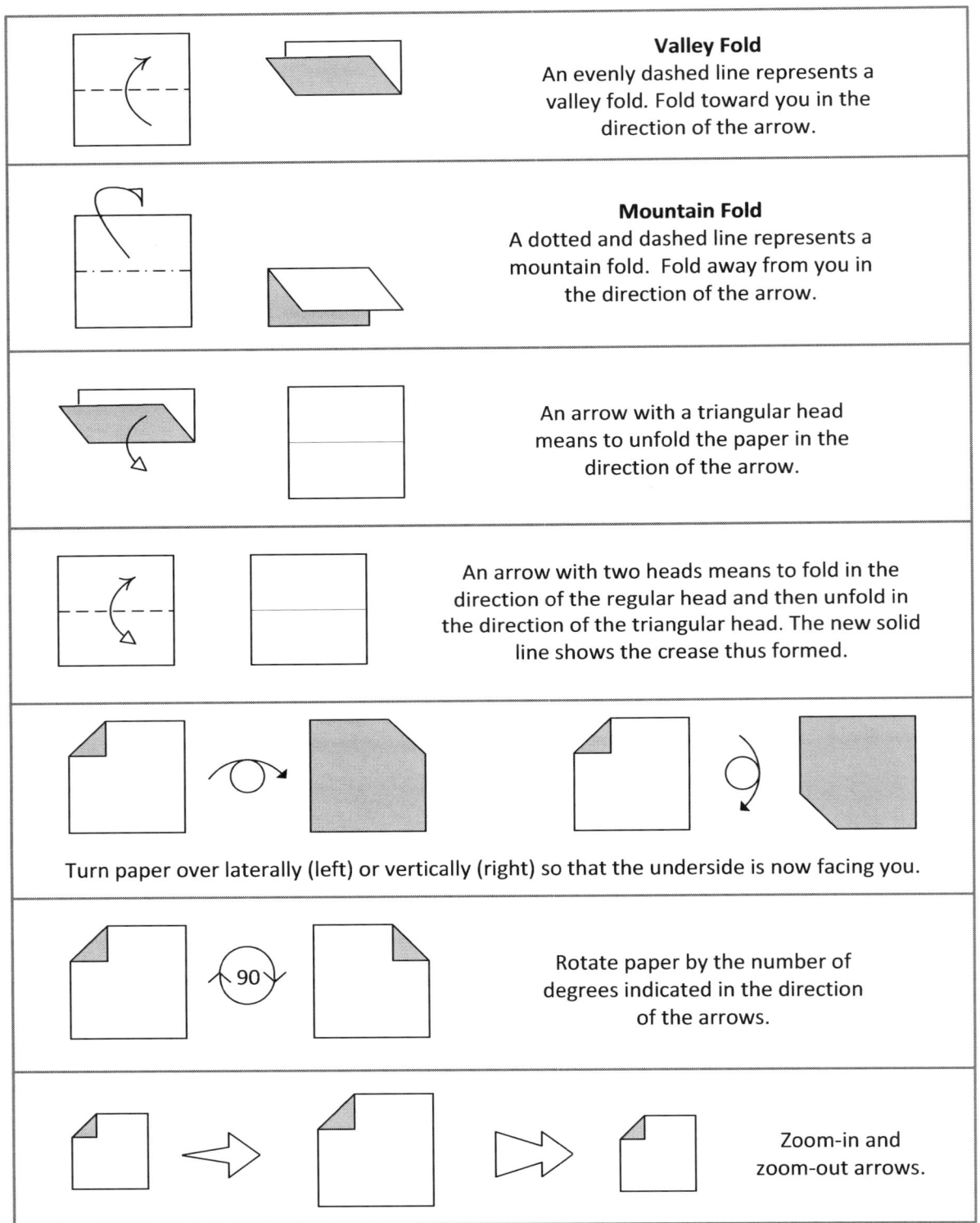

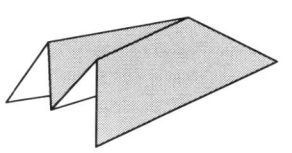 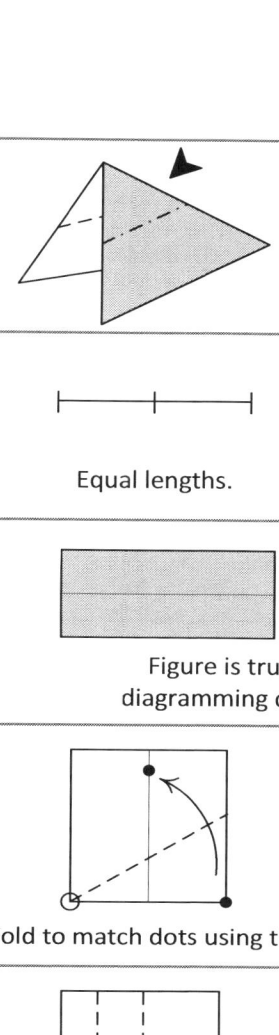

Sink or Reverse Fold or Inside Reverse Fold
Push in the direction of the arrow to arrive at the result.

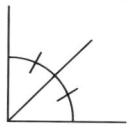

Equal lengths. Equal angles. A fold shown in X-ray vision, i.e., it is behind layers. 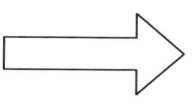 Pull out paper.

Figure is truncated for diagramming convenience.

Repeat once, twice, or as many times as indicated by the tail of the arrow.

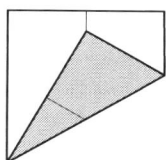

Fold to match dots using the circled point as pivot.

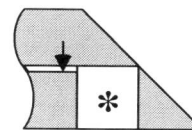 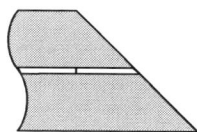

∗ : Tuck in opening underneath.

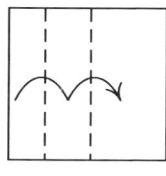 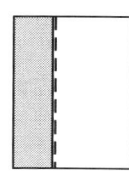 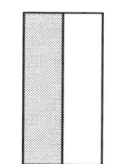

Fold repeatedly to arrive at the result.

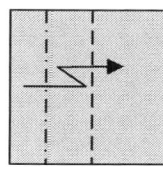    **Pleat Fold**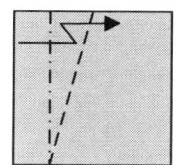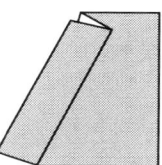

An alternate mountain and valley fold to form a pleat. Two examples are shown.

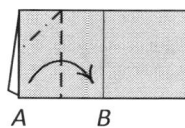 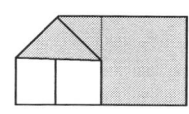

Squash Fold
Turn paper to the right along the valley fold while making the mountain crease such that A finally lies on B.

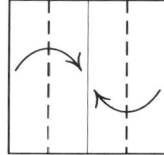 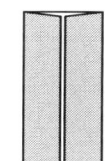

Cupboard Fold
First fold and unfold the centerfold, also called the **book-fold**, then valley fold the left and right edges to the center like cupboard doors.

Exquisite Modular Origami II

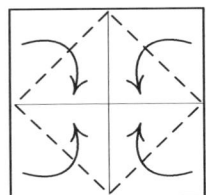 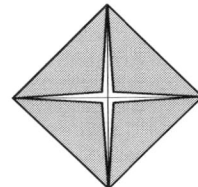

Blintz Base: Valley fold and unfold both book-folds. Then valley fold all four corners to the center.

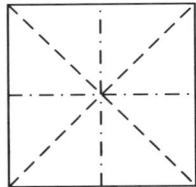 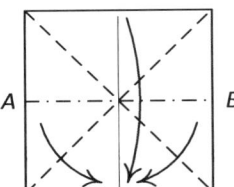 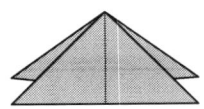

Waterbomb Base
Valley fold and unfold diagonals, then mountain fold and unfold book-folds. 'Break' line AB at the center and collapse such that A meets B.

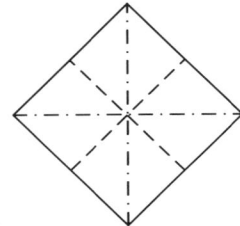 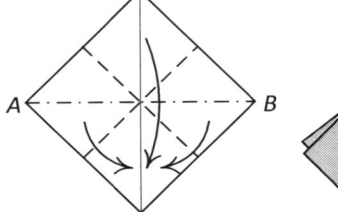 

Preliminary Base
This is similar to the waterbomb base above, but the mountain and valley folds are reversed, i.e., the diagonals are mountain folded and the book-folds are valley folded at start.

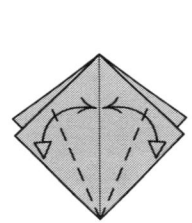 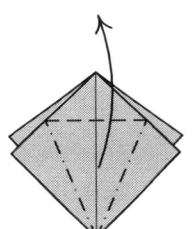 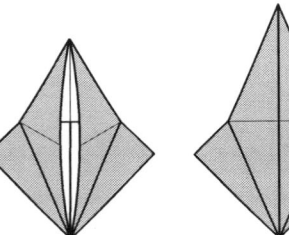

Petal Fold
The figure on the left illustrates petal folding on a flap of a preliminary base.

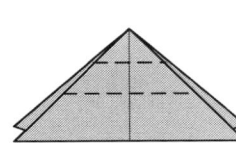 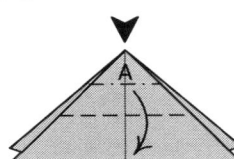 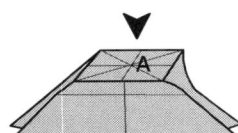 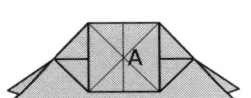

Spread Squash: Figure shows spread squashing the tip of a waterbomb base along the two valley creases shown. Note the final position of tip A after the squash.

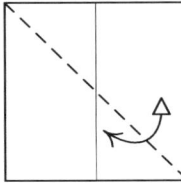 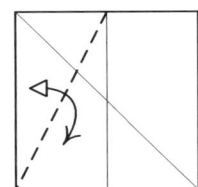 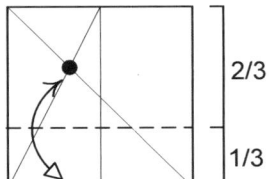 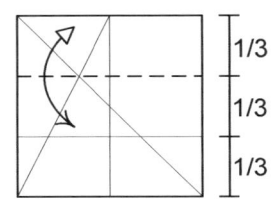

Folding A Square into Thirds: Crease book-fold and one diagonal. Crease diagonal of left rectangle to find 1/3 point. Bring bottom edge to this point and top edge to new line.

Exquisite Modular Origami II

Obtaining Rectangles from Squares (Only the proportions used in this book are shown here.)

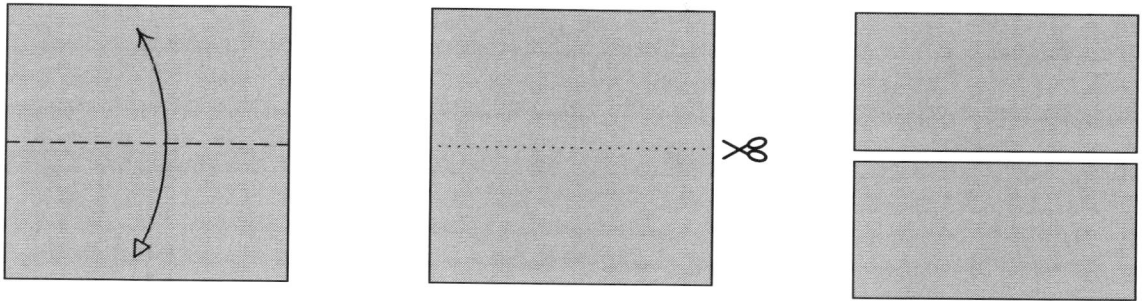

1:2 Rectangles – Fold in half and unfold. Cut along crease to get 1:2 rectangles.

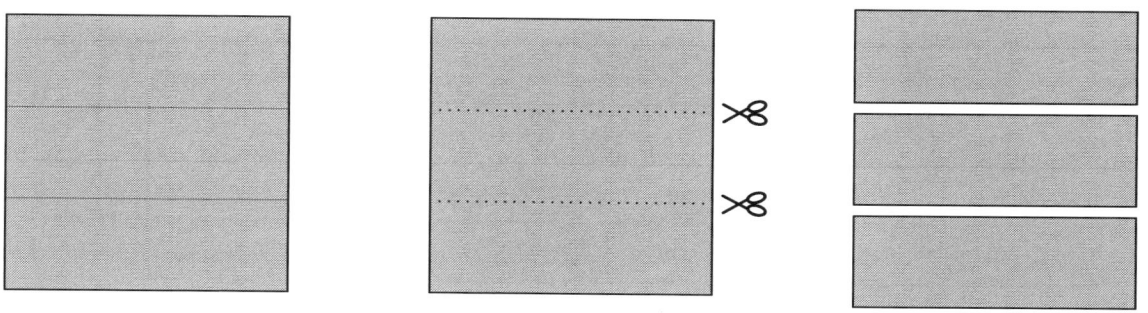

1:3 Rectangles – Fold in thirds using your favorite method or as shown on previous page. Cut along creases to get 1:3 rectangles. You can fold a template first to avoid unwanted creases.

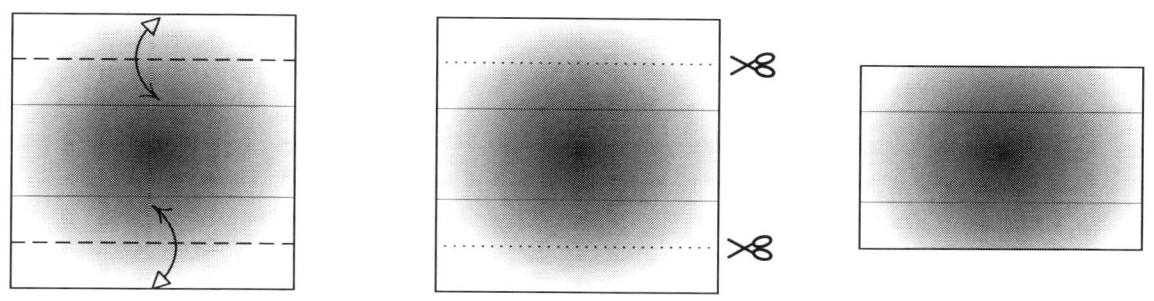

2:3 Rectangles – Fold like 1:3 rectangles but cut off only one of the thirds. For corona harmony paper, cut off a sixth from each edge as shown to have the corona centered.

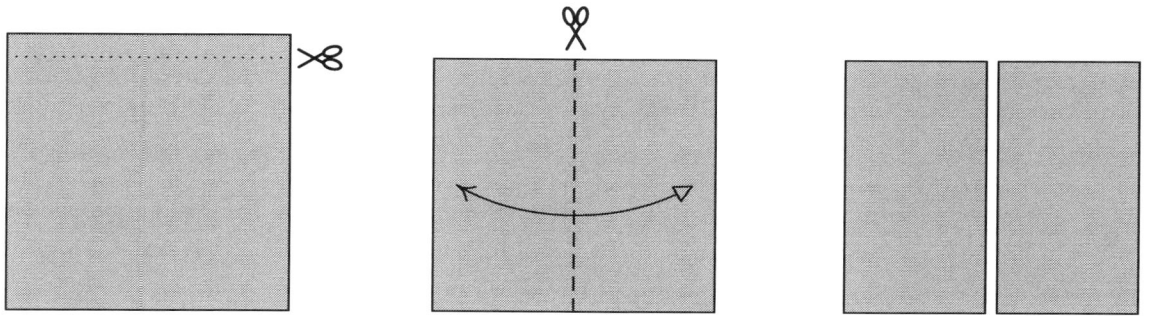

3"x5.5" Rectangles – Start with a 6" square and cut off half an inch. Then fold your rectangle in half as shown and cut along crease to get 3"x5.5" rectangles.

Platonic, Archimedean and Kepler-Poinsot Solids

Shown below are sets of polyhedra commonly referenced during origami constructions.

The Platonic solids, named after the ancient Greek philosopher Plato (428-348 BC), also called the regular solids, are convex polyhedra bound by faces that are congruent regular convex polygons. The same numbers of faces meet at each vertex. There are exactly five.

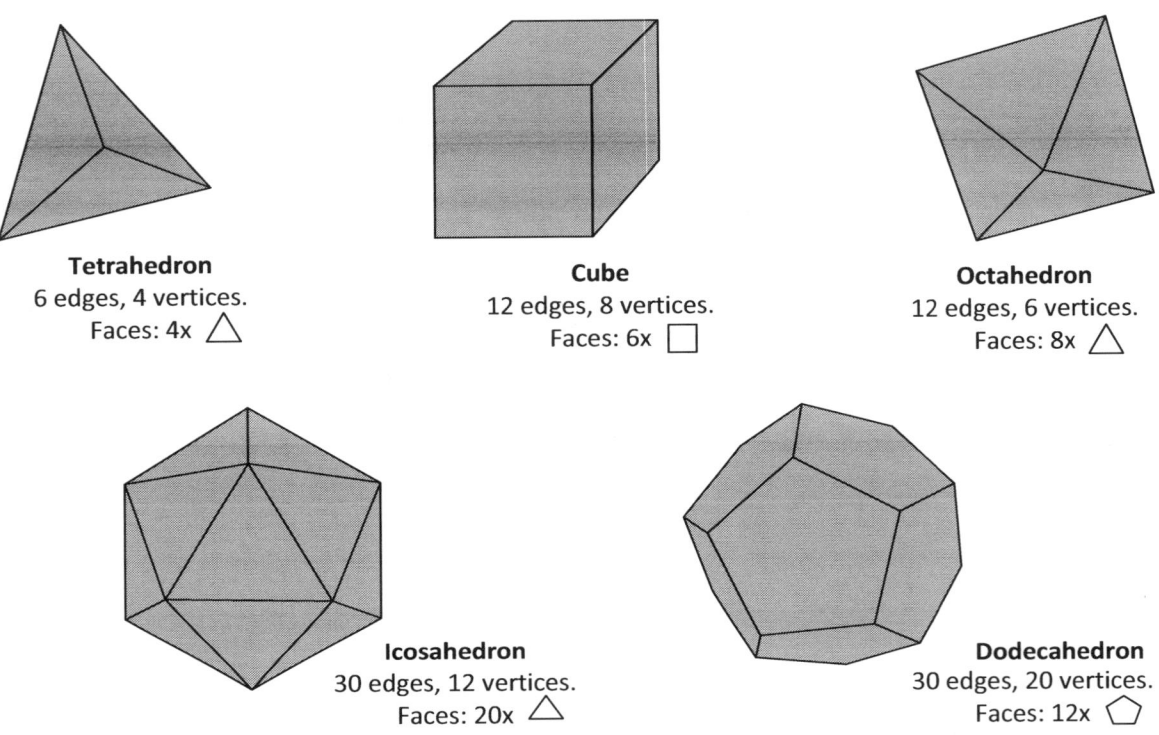

The Archimedean solids, named after Archimedes (287-212 BC), are semi-regular convex polyhedra bound by two or more types of regular convex polygons meeting in identical vertices. They are distinct from the Platonic solids which are composed of a single type of polygon meeting at identical vertices. Shown here are 8 of the 13 Archimedean solids. Those not shown are the Snub Dodecahedron, Truncated Tetrahedron, Truncated Dodecahedron, Great Rhombicosidodecahedron and Great Rhombicuboctahedron.

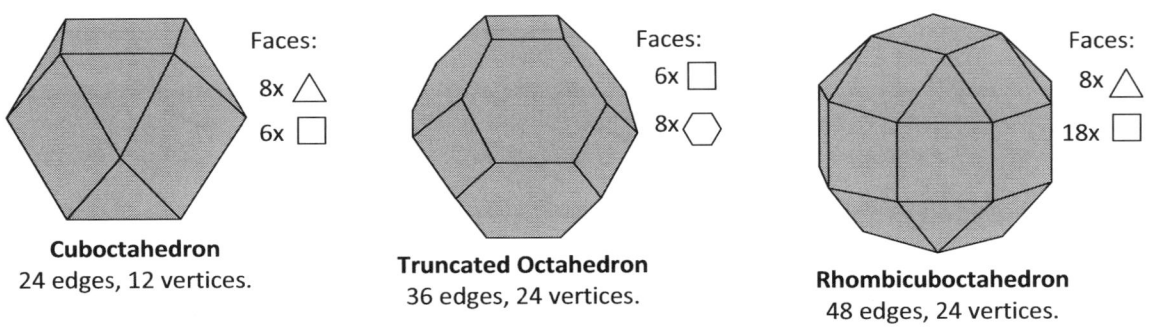

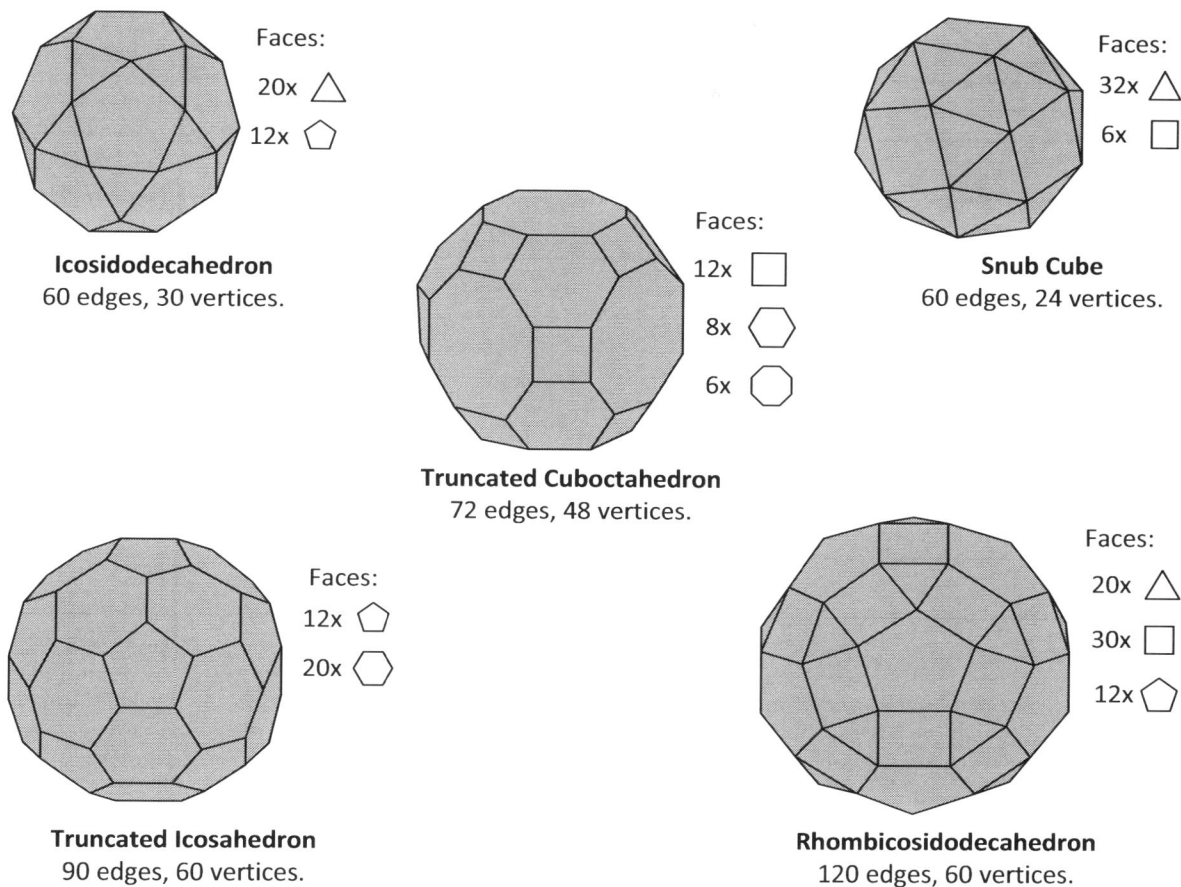

Icosidodecahedron
60 edges, 30 vertices.

Faces:
20x △
12x ⬠

Truncated Cuboctahedron
72 edges, 48 vertices.

Faces:
12x □
8x ⬡
6x ⯃

Snub Cube
60 edges, 24 vertices.

Faces:
32x △
6x □

Truncated Icosahedron
90 edges, 60 vertices.

Faces:
12x ⬠
20x ⬡

Rhombicosidodecahedron
120 edges, 60 vertices.

Faces:
20x △
30x □
12x ⬠

The Kepler-Poinsot solids, named after Johannes Kepler and Louis Poinsot (17th -19th century), are four regular concave polyhedra with intersecting facial planes. These can be obtained by stellating Platonic solids. Only two of the four are shown below. The two not shown are the Great Dodecahedron and the Great Icosahedron.

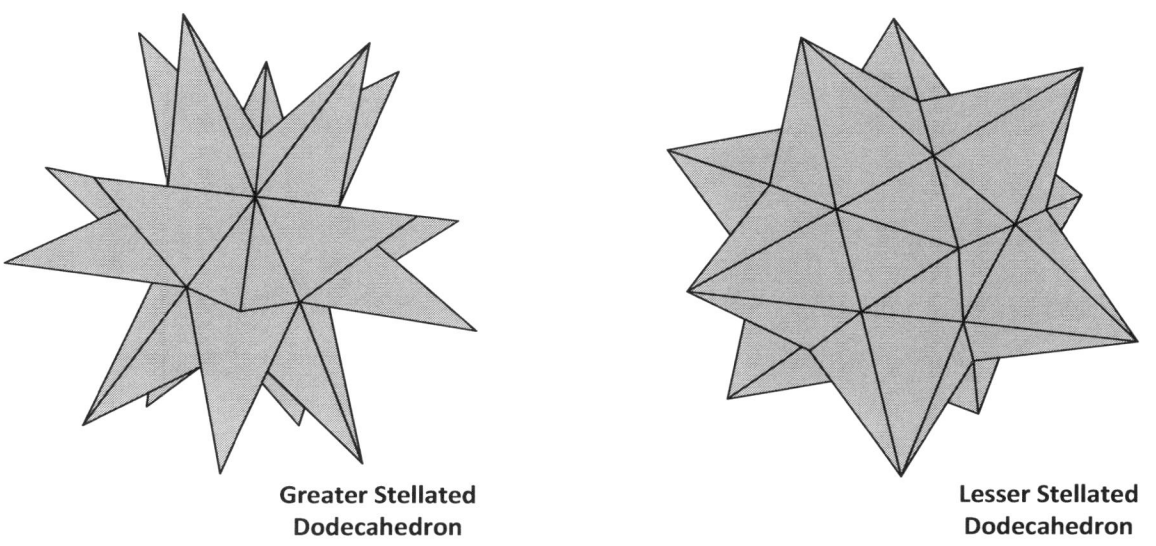

Greater Stellated Dodecahedron

Lesser Stellated Dodecahedron

Exquisite Modular Origami II

Hearty Cube and Variations

(Created April 2014)

This design is inspired by Francis Ow's Love Cube and Fumiaki Shingu's Heart Sonobe.

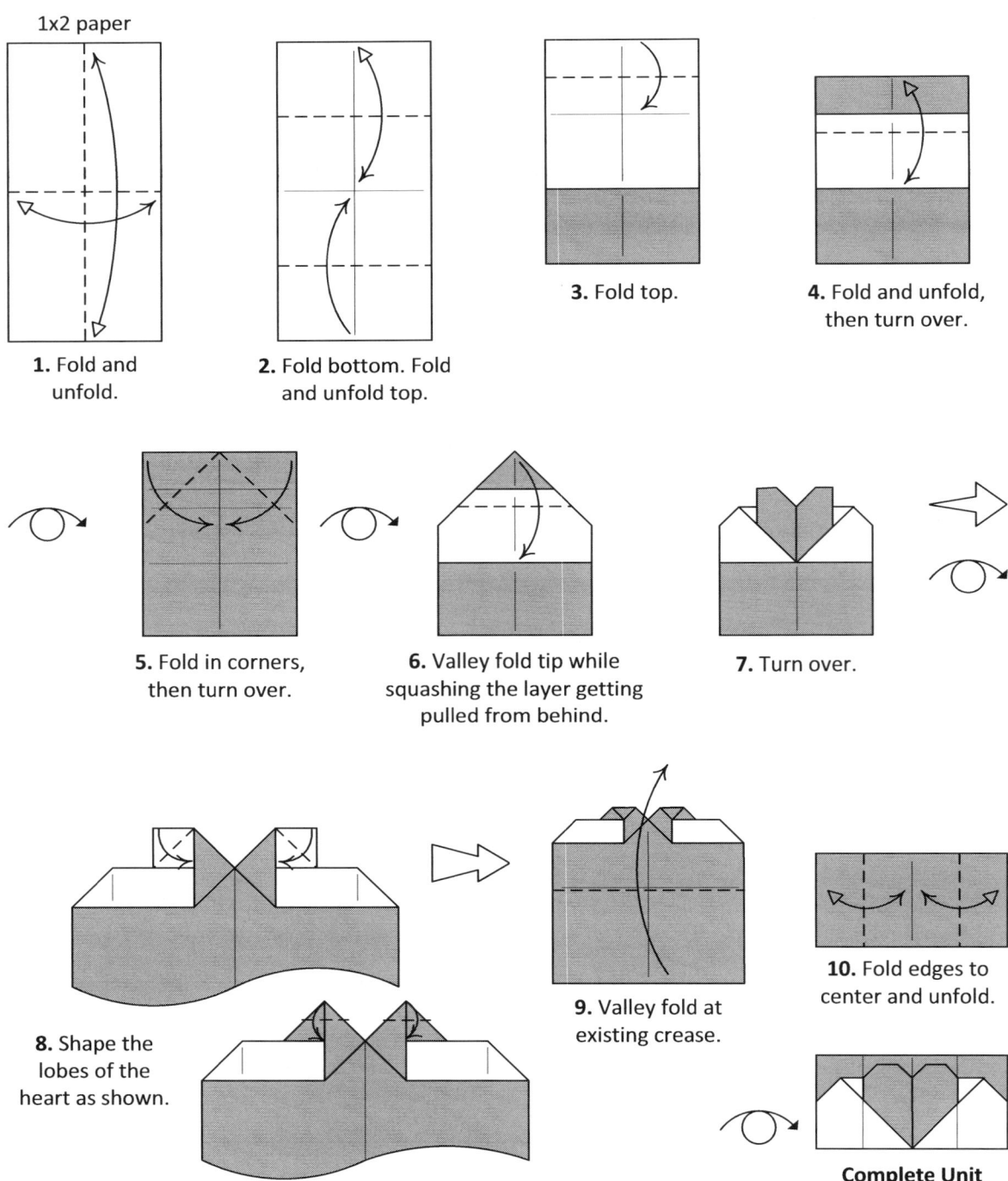

Exquisite Modular Origami II

Assembly

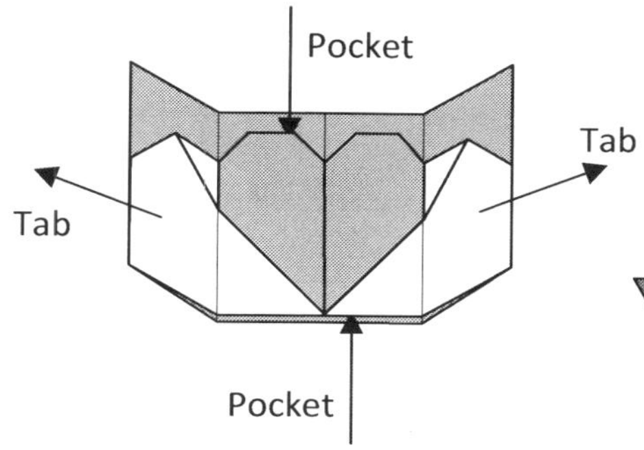

Join 5 units as shown. Finish by joining a 6th unit similarly. This assembly has 2 colored corners diagonally opposite to each other. The other 6 corners are white. You may assemble in other ways as well.

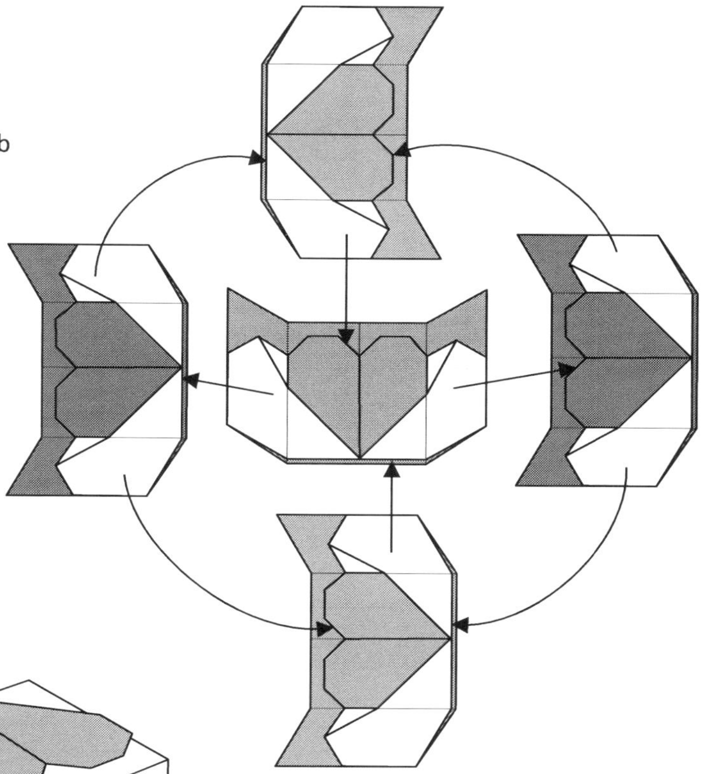

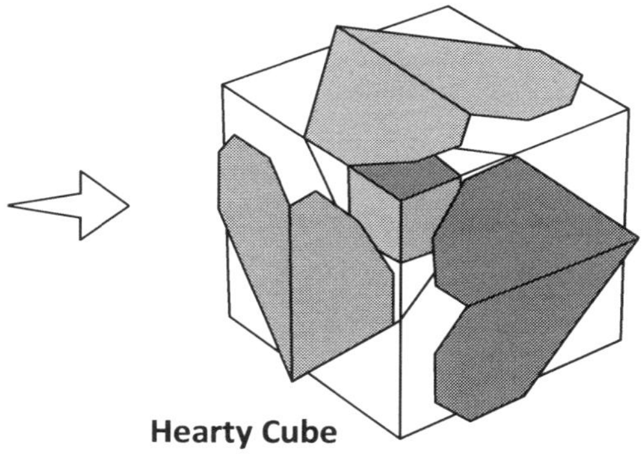

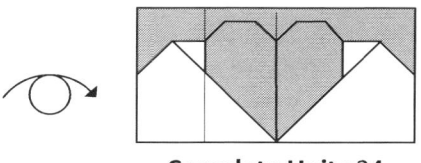

Hearty Cube

(Photo on back cover, third row, second from left)

24-Unit Colored Corner Assembly

Complete up to Step 9 of Hearty Cube.

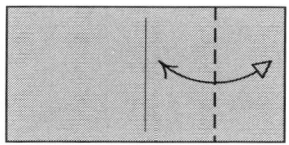

10'. Fold right edge to center and unfold.

Complete Unit x24

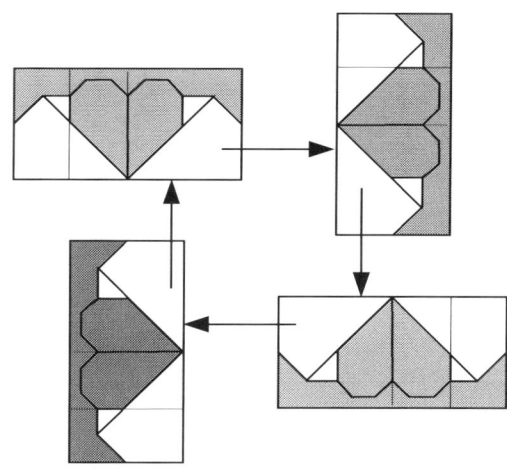

For a colored corner assembly, assemble 4 units as shown to form a face of the cube.

Exquisite Modular Origami II

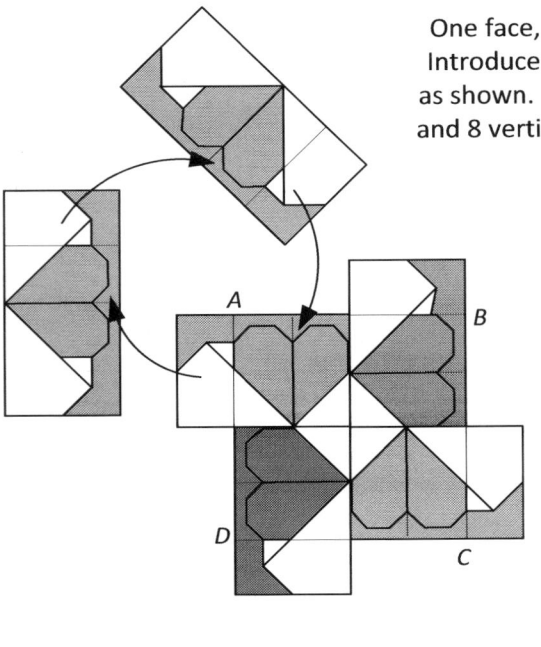

One face, *ABCD,* of the cube is now formed. Introduce 2 more units to form a vertex at A as shown. Continue forming a total of 6 faces and 8 vertices similarly, to complete the cube.

24-Unit White Corner Assembly

Fold the units same as the colored corner assembly.

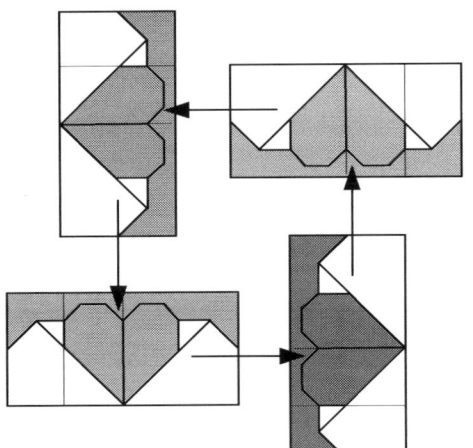

Assemble just like the colored corner cube but orient the units as shown.

Note: During assembly, the 24-unit cubes are a bit unstable but the overall structures are stable, though they need careful handling. The assemblies are a fun challenge because your fingers have to move skillfully around while your palms hold the assembly like a cup.

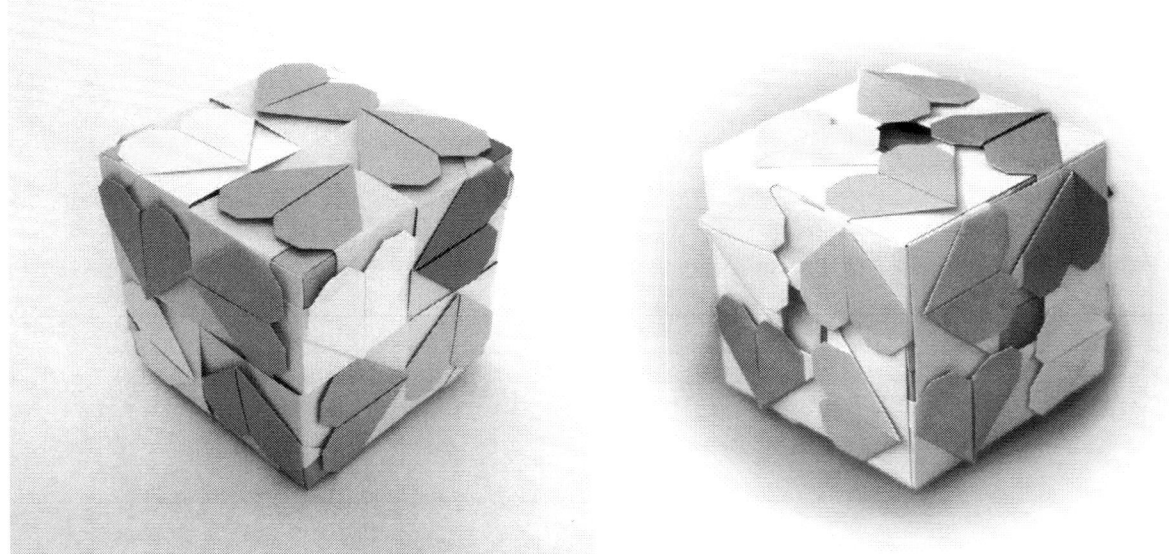

24-Unit Hearty Cube Assemblies, Colored Corners and White Corners

Exquisite Modular Origami II

Decorative Cube and Variations
(Created June 2014)

The Decorative Cubes are an improvement over my previous Windmill Base Cubes from 2009 (*Origami Inspirations*, [Muk10]) in that, no separate joining tabs are needed. Each face is still a Froebel type design but the use of separate joining tabs is eliminated by starting with Blintzed Windmill Bases instead of ordinary Windmill Bases. Corona Harmony paper, 6" or larger, best suits the design though solid paper works well too.

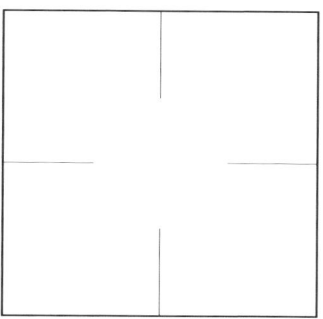

1. Book-fold both ways. Do not crease near the center.

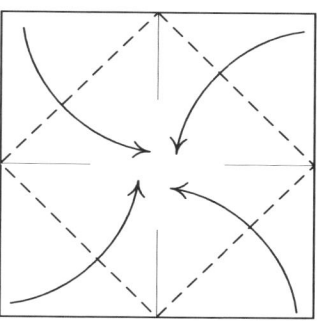

2. Blintz fold.

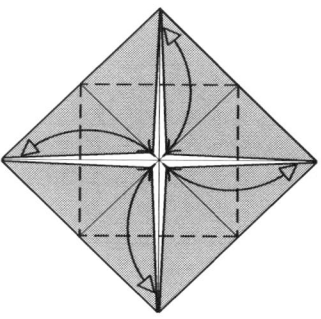

3. Blintz fold through all layers and unfold. Turn over and rotate.

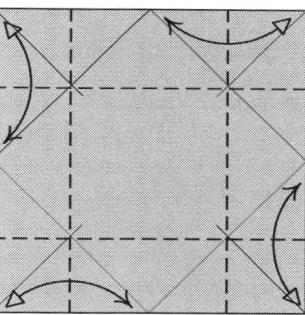

4. Cupboard fold both ways through all layers and unfold.

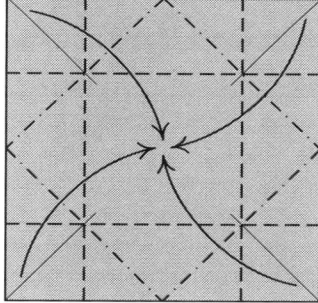

5. Collapse into a windmill base following the gender of the folds.

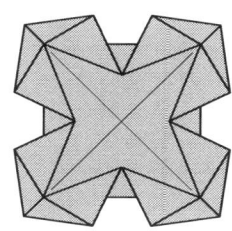

6. Collapse in progress. Flatten completely to arrive at the Blintz Windmill Base.

7. The flat result. Fold the four inside corners out.

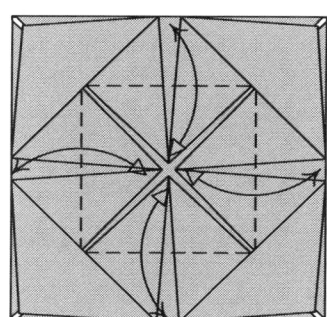

8. Fold the other set of four inner corners to edge (or less) and unfold.

Exquisite Modular Origami II

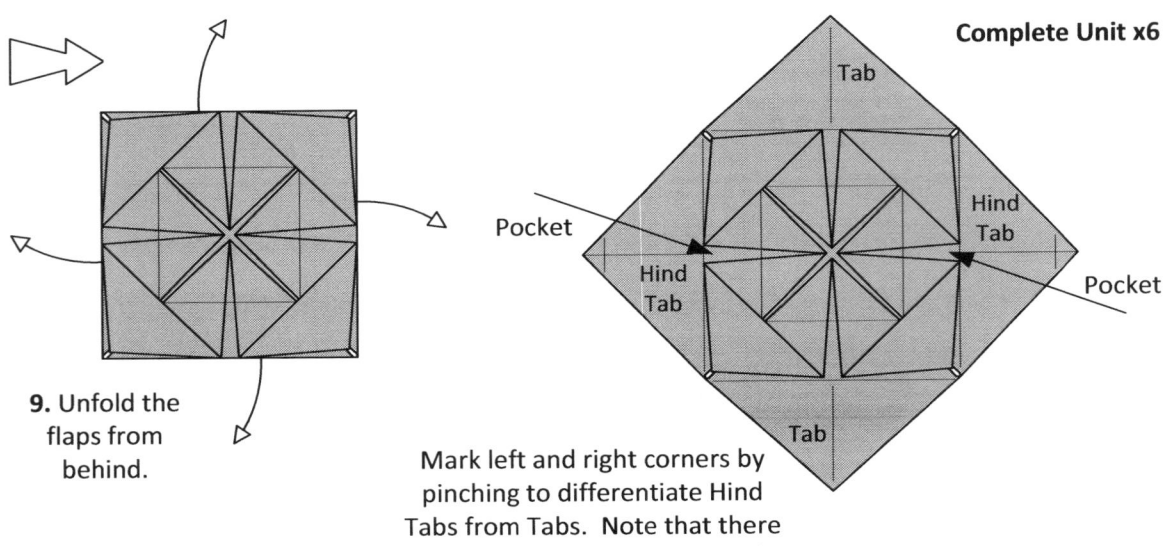

9. Unfold the flaps from behind.

Complete Unit x6

Mark left and right corners by pinching to differentiate Hind Tabs from Tabs. Note that there are Hind Pockets behind the Tabs.

Assembly

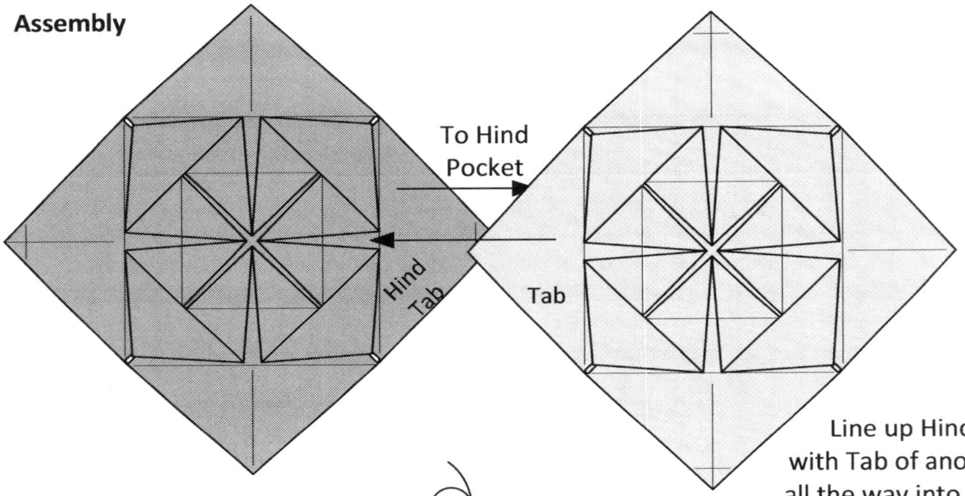

Line up Hind Tab of one unit with Tab of another unit. Insert all the way into Pocket and Hind Pocket, making sure that the Tab is in front of the Hind Tab.

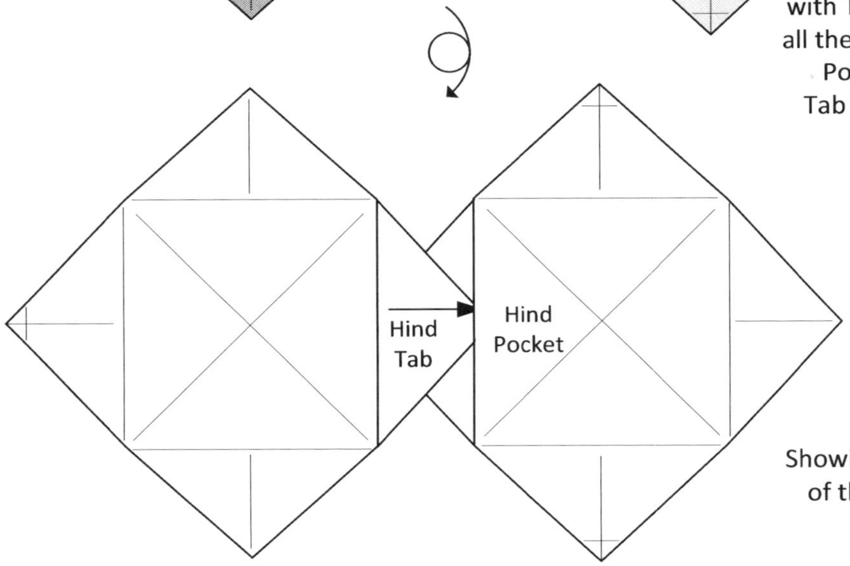

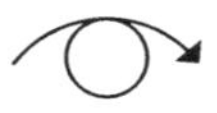

Showing the rear side of the insertion in progress.

Exquisite Modular Origami II

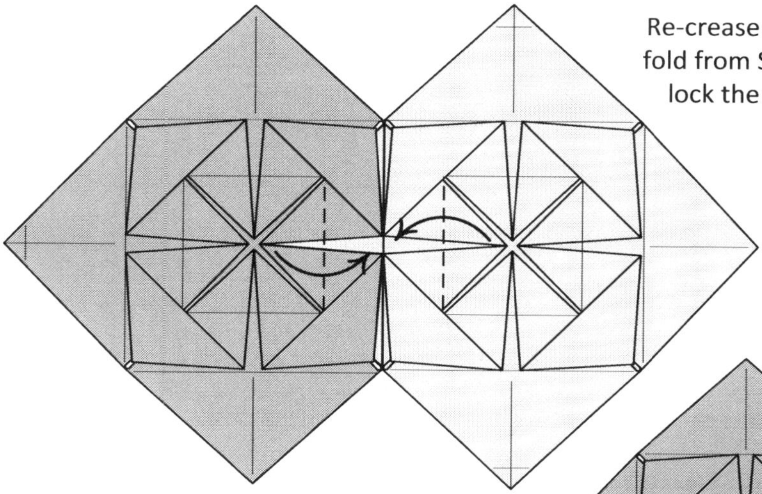

Re-crease two of the valley fold from Step 9 to securely lock the units together.

Two units locked.

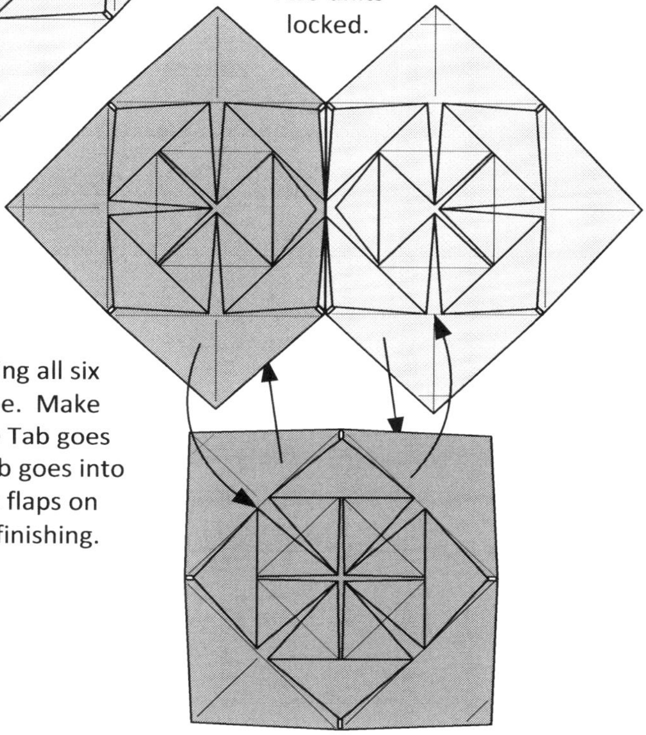

Continue joining and locking all six faces to complete the cube. Make sure that for each joint the Tab goes into Pocket and the Hind Tab goes into Hind Pocket. Curl all eight flaps on each face of the cube for finishing.

Note: Shown next are a few variations of the Decorative Cube. You are encouraged to try other Froebel type variations by applying them to Blintzed Windmill Bases and connecting them as explained here.

Decorative Cube

(Photo on back cover, third row, left).

Exquisite Modular Origami II

Variation 1
Start with Step 7 of Decorative Cube flattened completely.

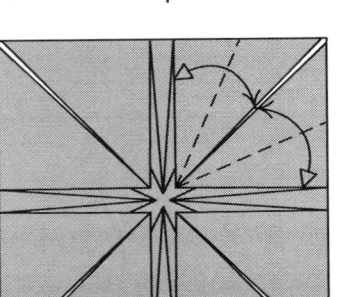
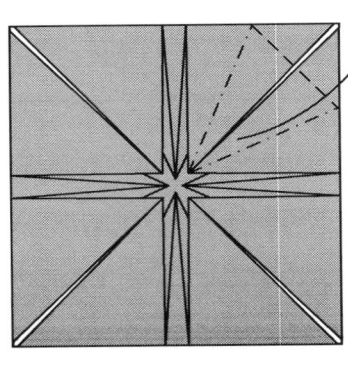
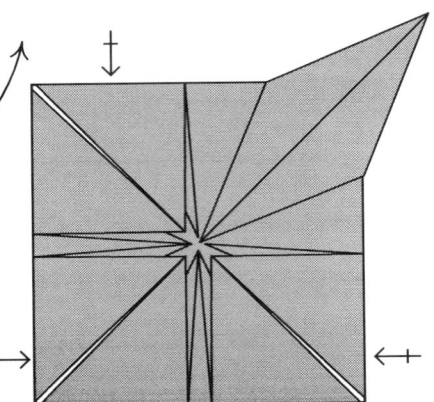

1. Fold the flap as shown and unfold.

2. Petal fold the flap.

3. Repeat Steps 1 and 2 on the other three corners.

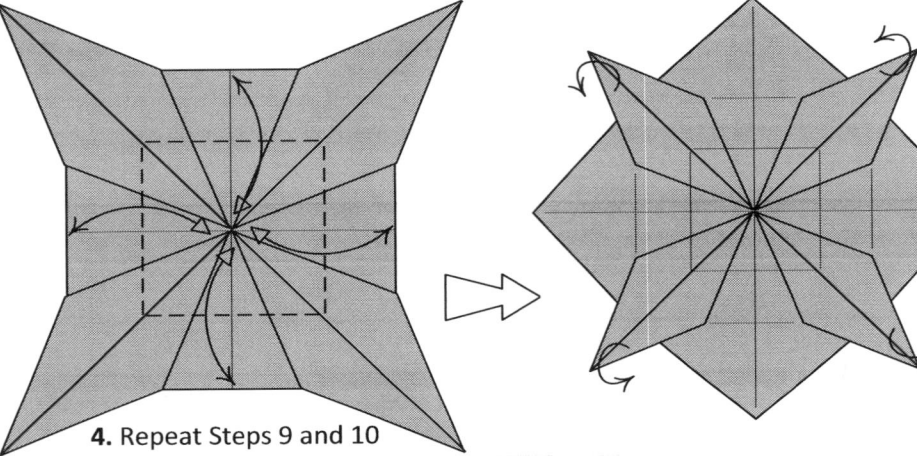

4. Repeat Steps 9 and 10 of Decorative Cube. You may crease a smaller inner square if you wish.

5. Curl the four tips toward you.

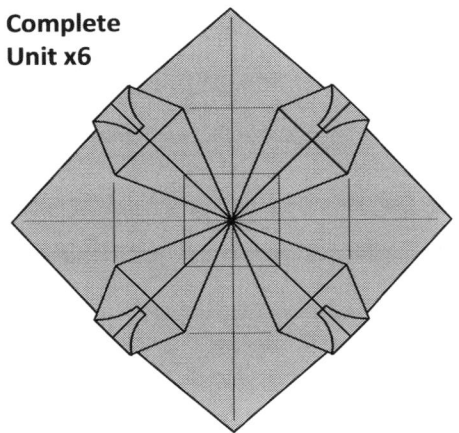

Complete Unit x6

Join six units inserting and locking exactly like Decorative Cube.

Decorative Cube Variation 1

Exquisite Modular Origami II

Variation 2

Start with a completed Variation 1 unit and open up the petals instead of curling.

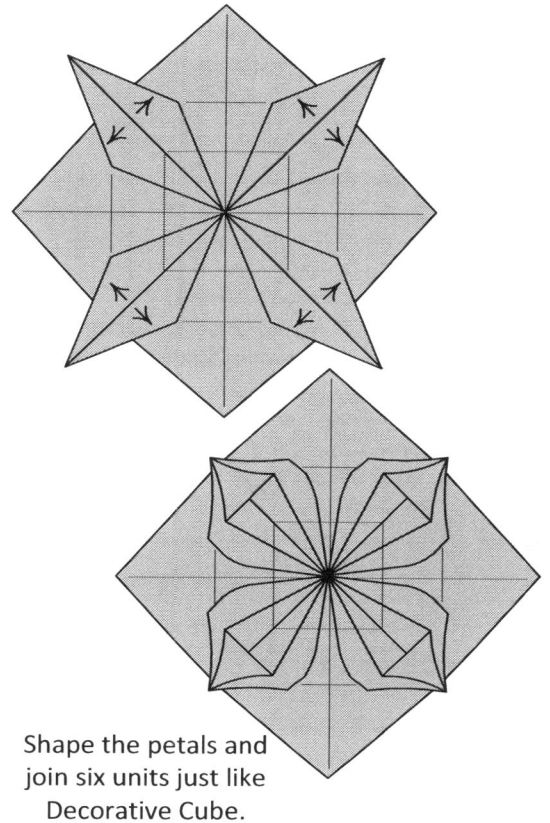

Shape the petals and join six units just like Decorative Cube.

Decorative Cube Variation 2

Variation 3

Start with Step 1 of Variation 1. Squash each of the eight flaps instead of petal folding.

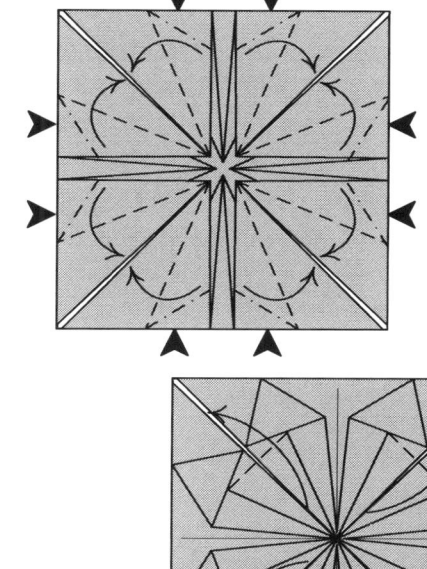

Fold the central tips out and continue with Step 9 onwards of Decorative Cube.

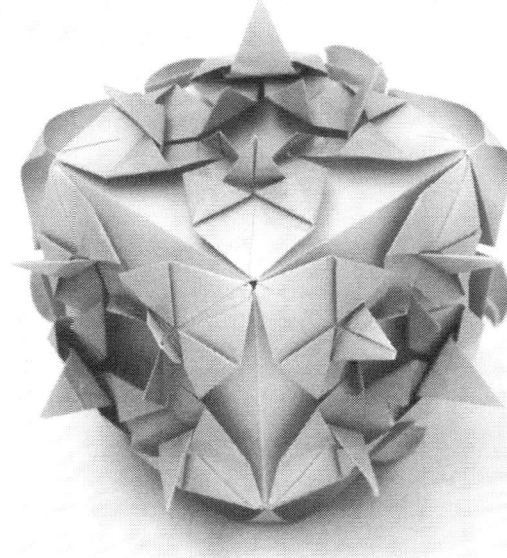

Decorative Cube Variation 3

Patterned Skeloctahedron and Variations

(Created April 2015)

These skeletal octahedra are inspired by Robert Neale's Waterbomb Base Ornament. Other variations are possible and folders are encouraged to try their hands at it.

Patterned Skeloctahedron 1

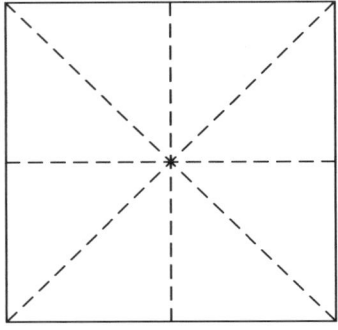
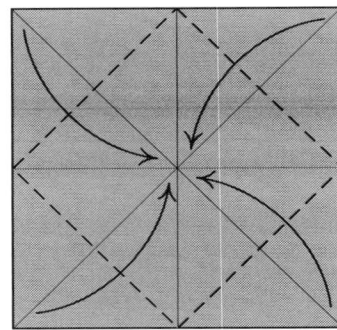
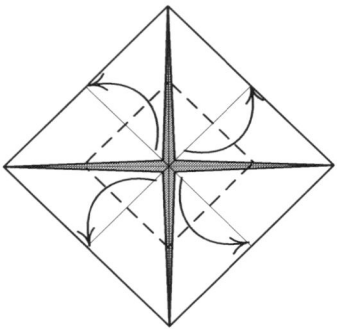

1. Crease book-folds and diagonals.　　**2.** Blintz fold.　　**3.** Fold corners out to edges.

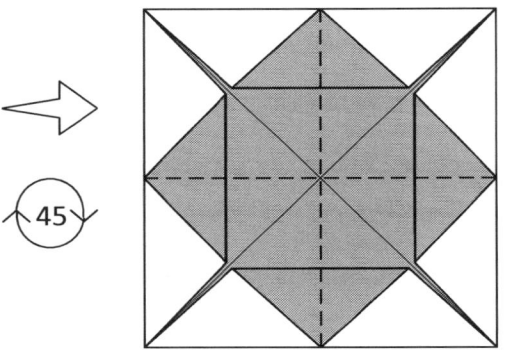
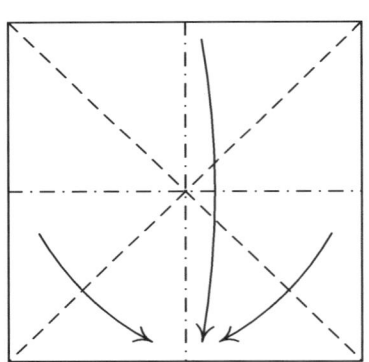

4. Reinforce valley folds through all layers.　　**5.** Collapse like a waterbomb base.

Finished Unit x6

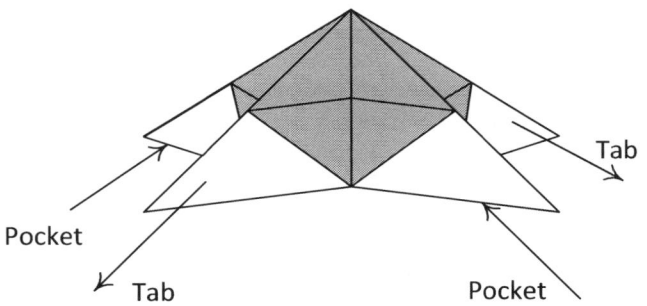

(Note how 2 opposite legs are pockets and the other two are tabs. It's very important to remember this during assembly.)

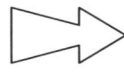

Exquisite Modular Origami II

Assembly

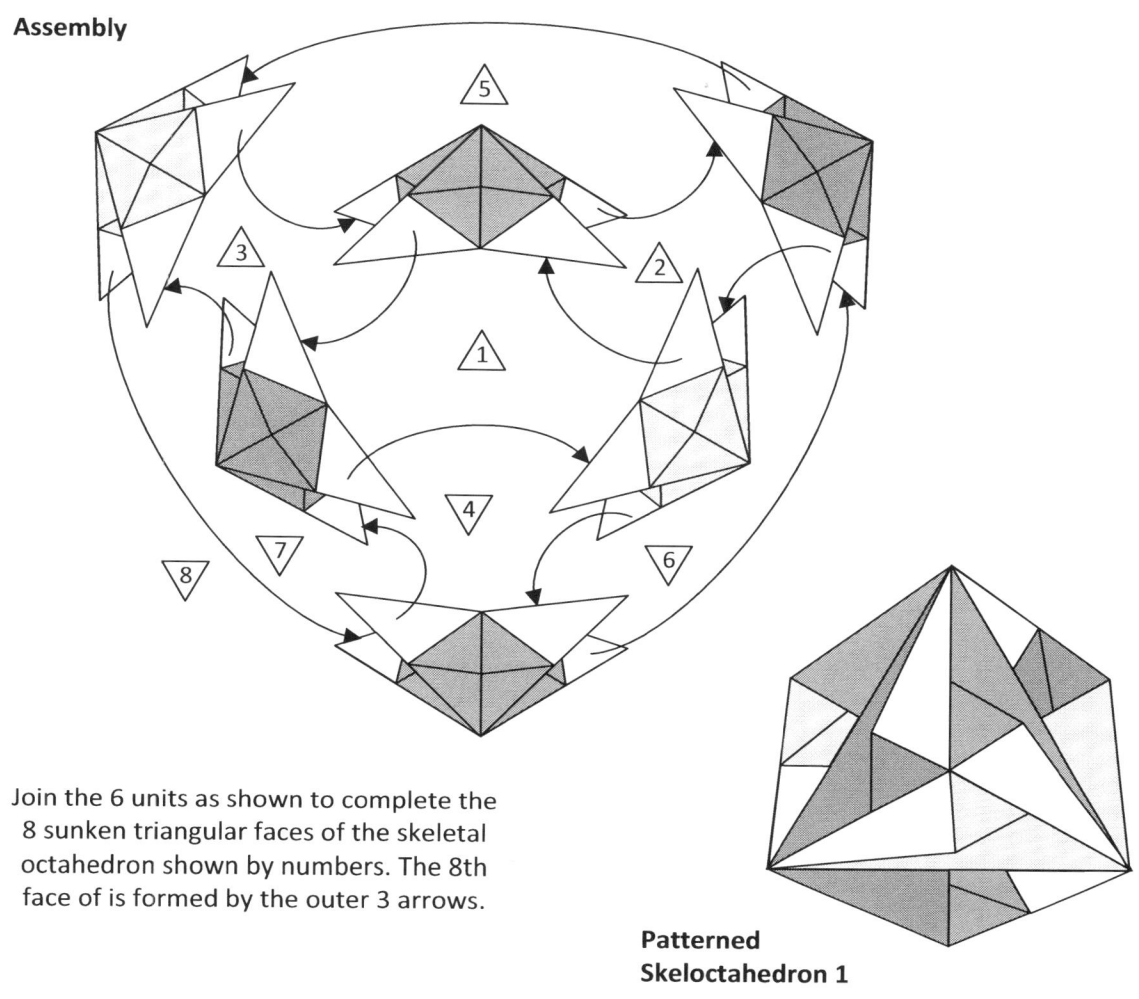

Join the 6 units as shown to complete the 8 sunken triangular faces of the skeletal octahedron shown by numbers. The 8th face of is formed by the outer 3 arrows.

Patterned Skeloctahedron 1

Patterned Skeloctahedron 2

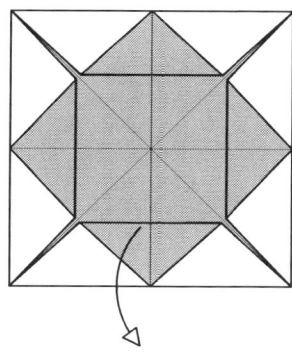

1. Start with Step 4 of Skeloctahedron 1 and unfold the flap shown.

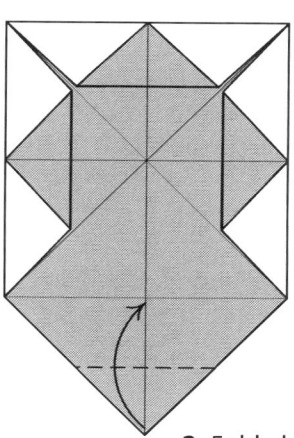

2. Fold along existing crease.

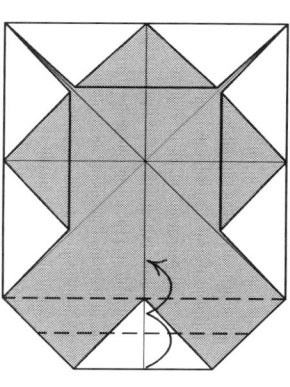

3. Fold repeatedly as shown.

Exquisite Modular Origami II

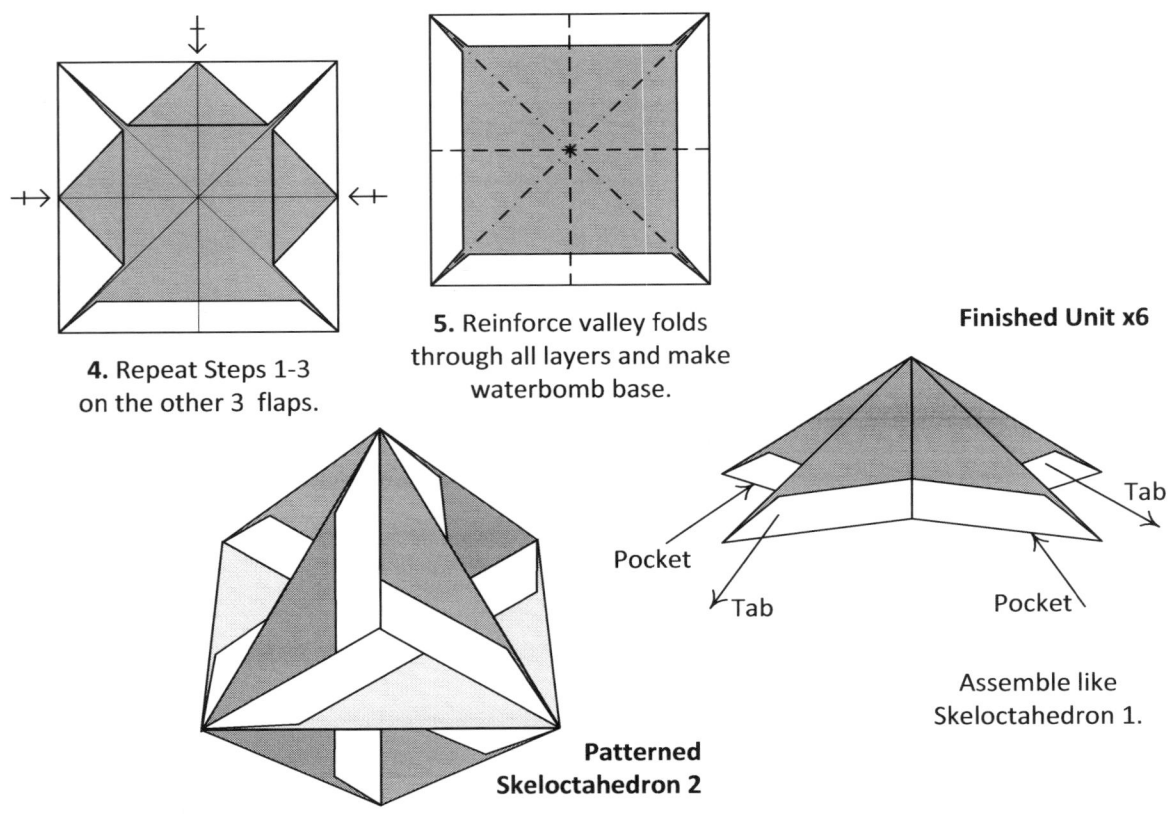

4. Repeat Steps 1-3 on the other 3 flaps.

5. Reinforce valley folds through all layers and make waterbomb base.

Finished Unit x6

Tab
Pocket
Tab
Pocket

Assemble like Skeloctahedron 1.

Patterned Skeloctahedron 2

Patterned Skeloctahedron 3

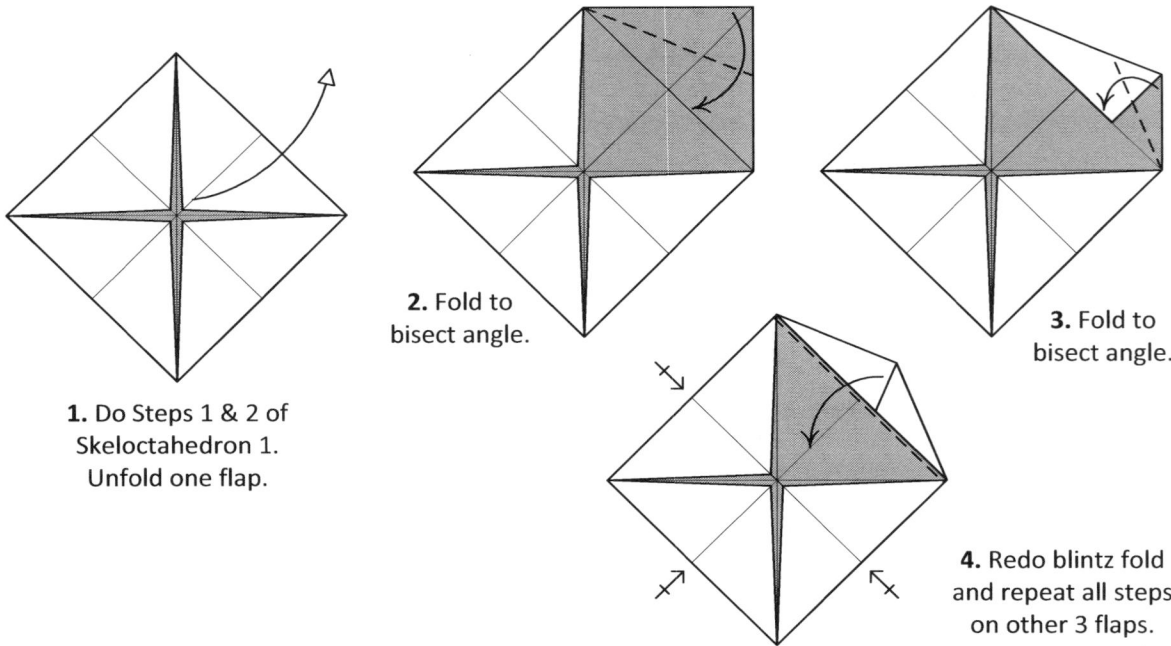

1. Do Steps 1 & 2 of Skeloctahedron 1. Unfold one flap.

2. Fold to bisect angle.

3. Fold to bisect angle.

4. Redo blintz fold and repeat all steps on other 3 flaps.

Exquisite Modular Origami II

20

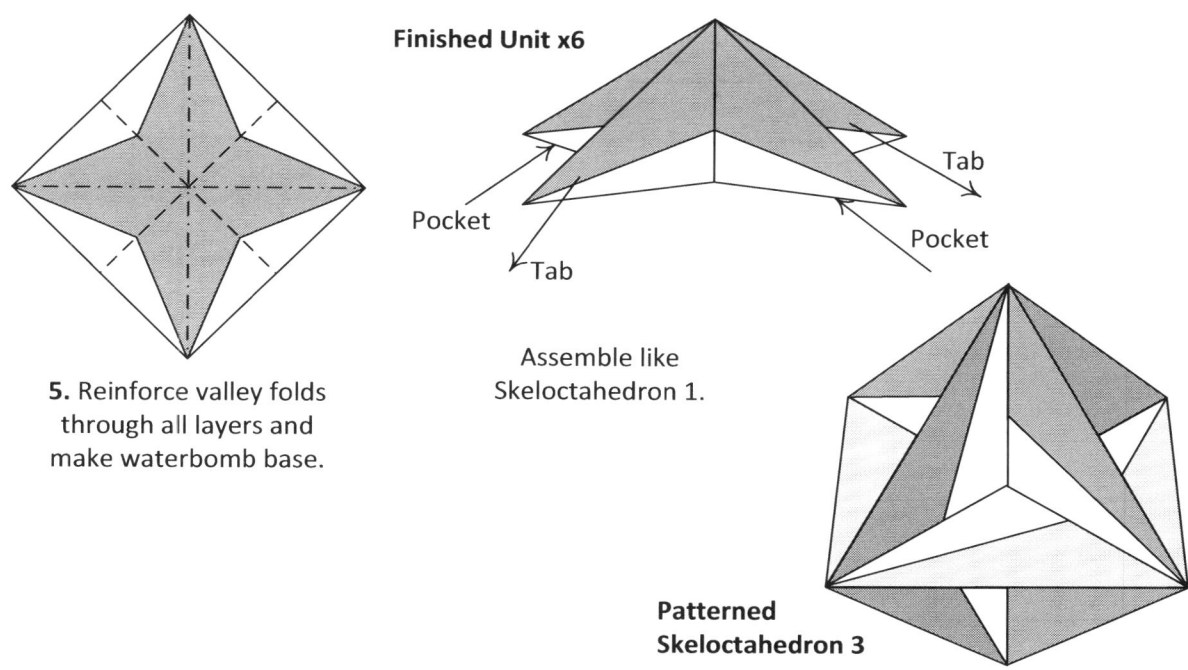

5. Reinforce valley folds through all layers and make waterbomb base.

Finished Unit x6

Assemble like Skeloctahedron 1.

Patterned Skeloctahedron 3

Patterned Skeloctahedron 4

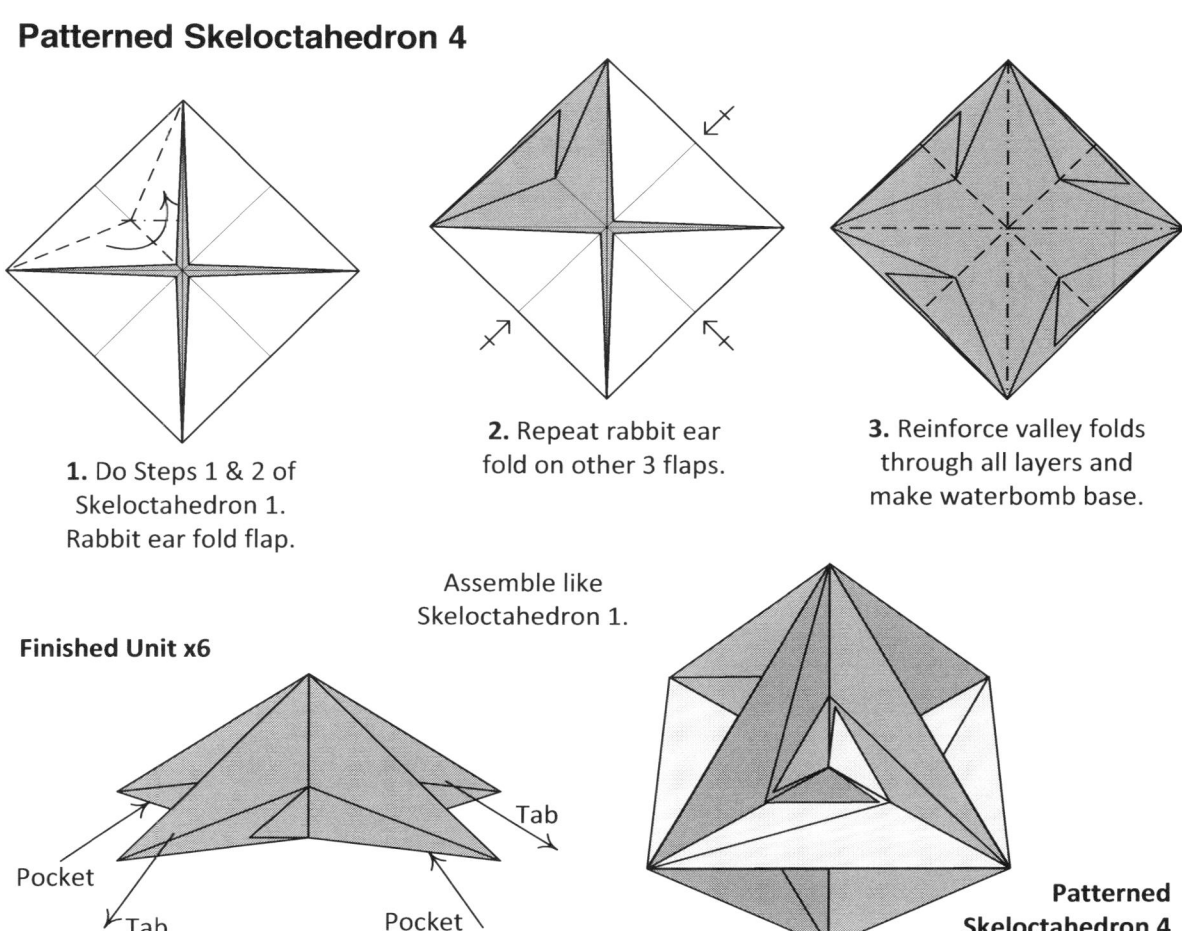

1. Do Steps 1 & 2 of Skeloctahedron 1. Rabbit ear fold flap.

2. Repeat rabbit ear fold on other 3 flaps.

3. Reinforce valley folds through all layers and make waterbomb base.

Finished Unit x6

Assemble like Skeloctahedron 1.

Patterned Skeloctahedron 4

Exquisite Modular Origami II

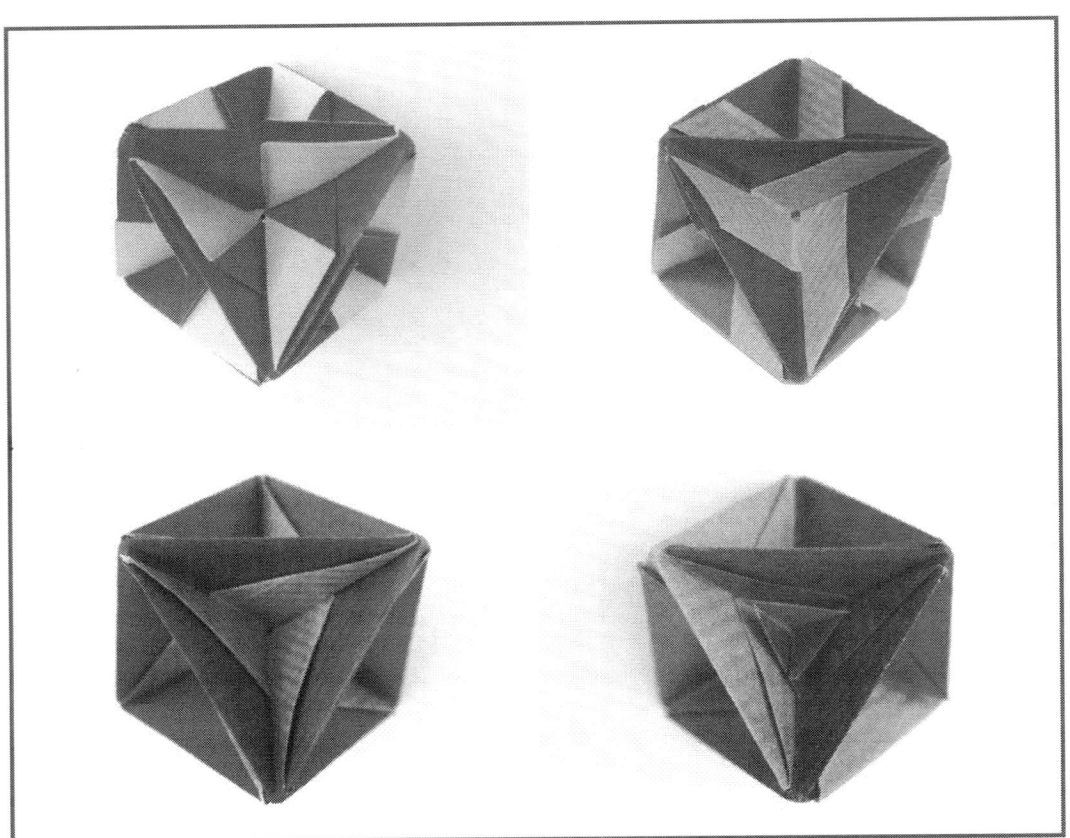

The Four Variations of Patterned Skeloctahedron.
Another photo on back cover, bottom right.

Flora (next page) in a split vane assembly.

Exquisite Modular Origami II

Flora
(Created July 2014)

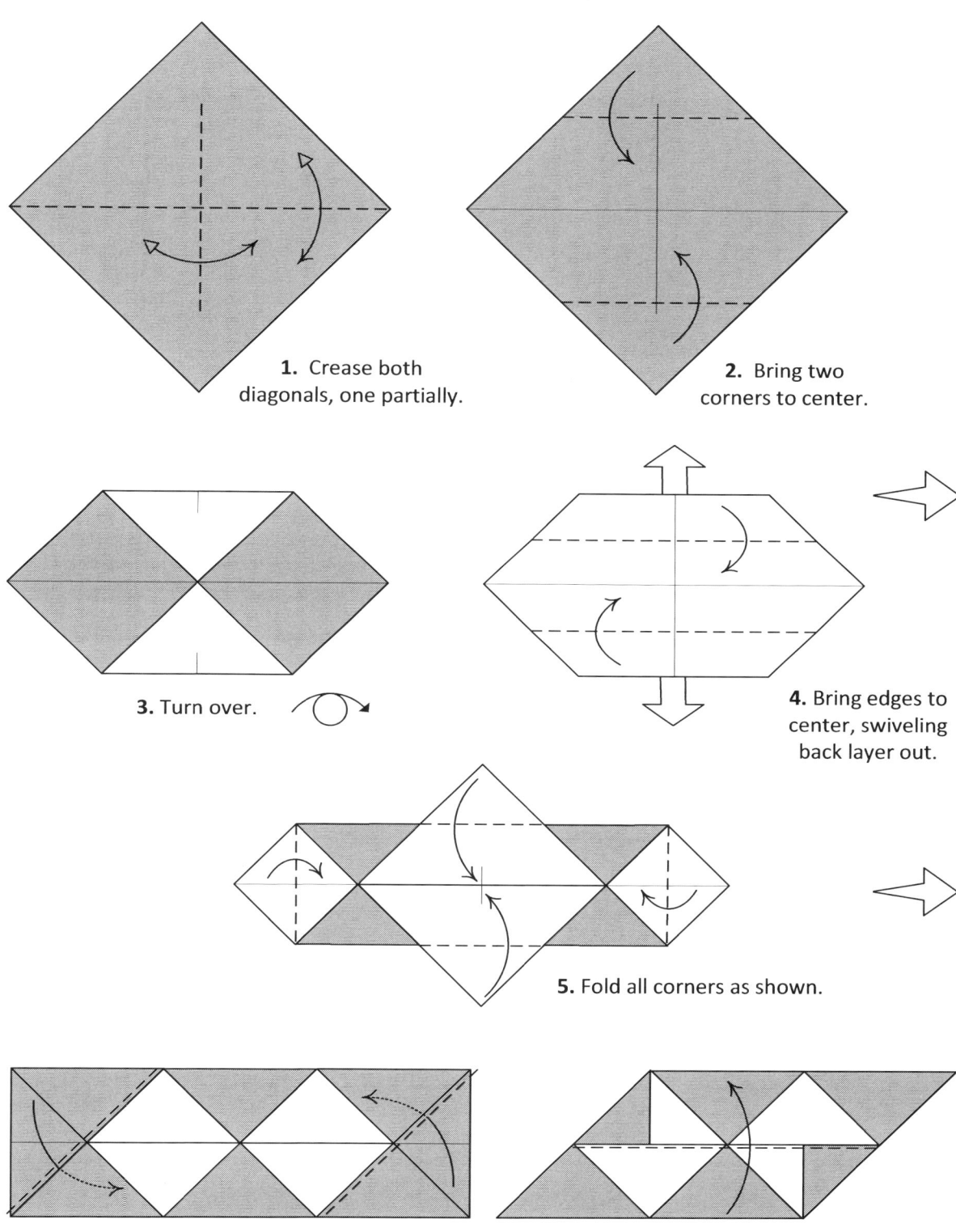

1. Crease both diagonals, one partially.
2. Bring two corners to center.
3. Turn over.
4. Bring edges to center, swiveling back layer out.
5. Fold all corners as shown.
6. Fold and tuck under openings.
7. Fold in half through all layers.

Exquisite Modular Origami II

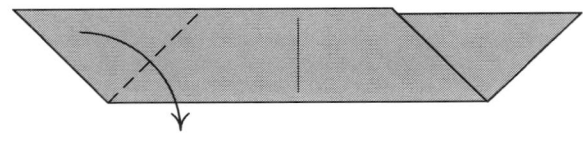

8. Fold along edge at the back.

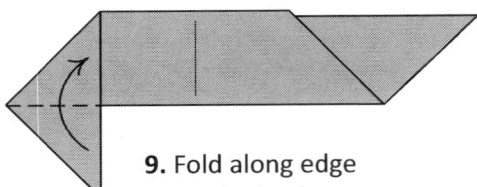

9. Fold along edge at the back.

10. Turn over and repeat on the other side.

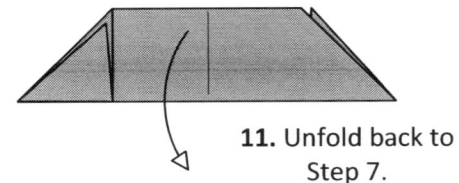

11. Unfold back to Step 7.

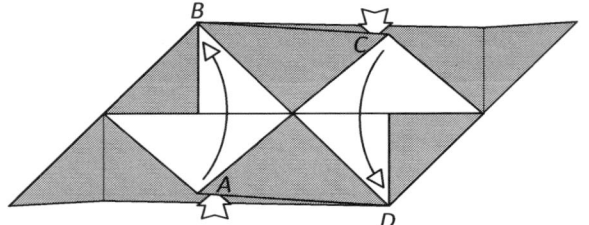

12. Lift point *A* and bring towards *B,* and point *C* towards *D*. The unit will now become 3D.

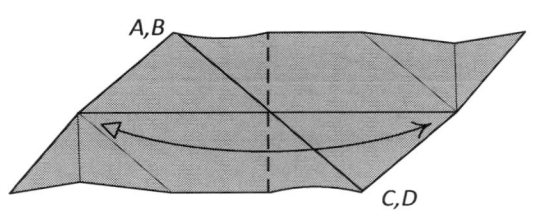

13. Fold and unfold without creasing the flaps/vanes at the center.

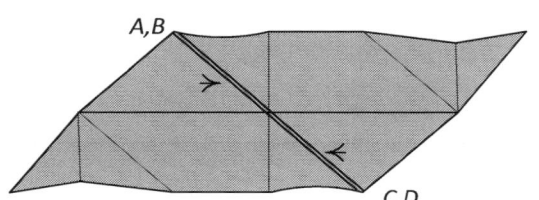

14. Using your nails, gently curve the central vanes together like an S.

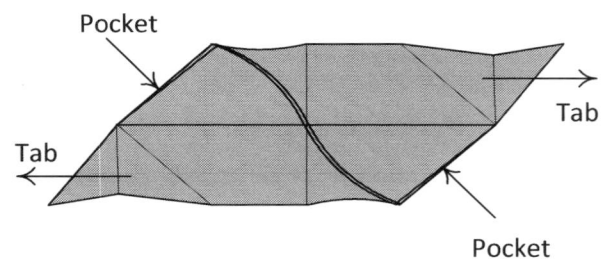

Finished Unit x30

Assembly

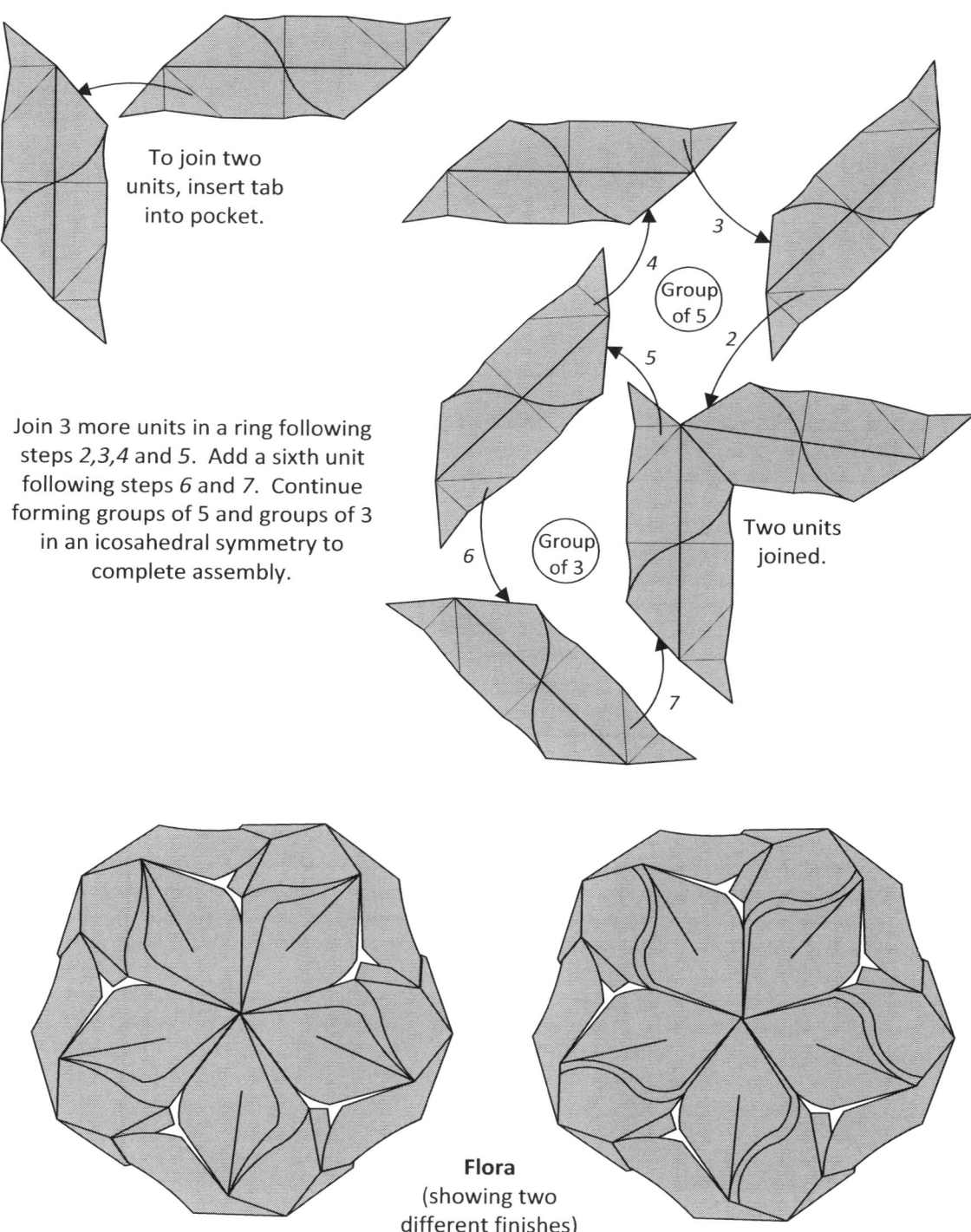

To join two units, insert tab into pocket.

Join 3 more units in a ring following steps *2,3,4* and *5*. Add a sixth unit following steps *6* and *7*. Continue forming groups of 5 and groups of 3 in an icosahedral symmetry to complete assembly.

Two units joined.

Flora
(showing two different finishes)

Note: The central vanes/flaps of the units tend to separate during assembly. You may leave them separated (left) or go around the finished model bringing them together again if you like (right).

(Photo on back cover, top row, second from right. More split vane assembly on page 22.)

Exquisite Modular Origami II

Curly Locks
(Created March 2012)

Naming this model has been fun and has nothing to do with hair-do! The tab and pocket pairs have been curled together to secure the locks and hence the name. This locking method is inspired by Byriah Loper's Blooming Curls. Use Corona Harmony Paper if you wish to have distinct colored petals.

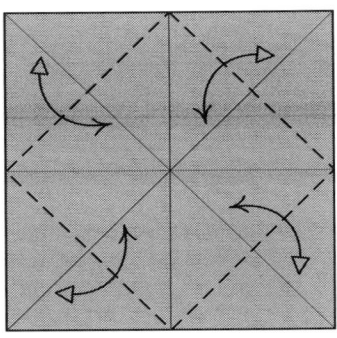

1. Valley fold both diagonals and book-folds and unfold, then blintz fold and unfold.

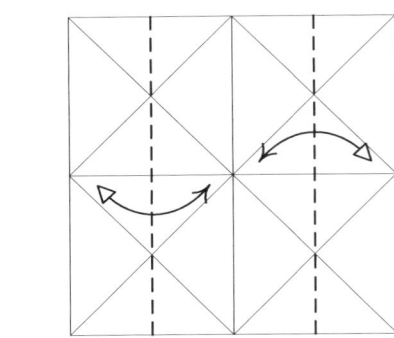

2. Cupboard fold and unfold. Rotate 90°.

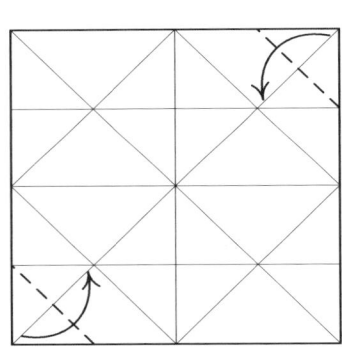

3. Valley fold corners.

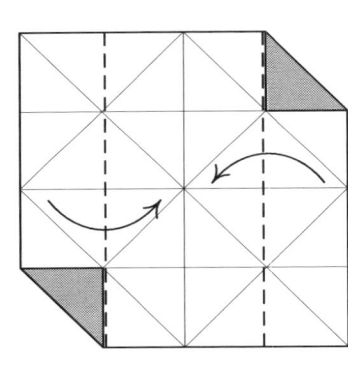

4. Cupboard fold.

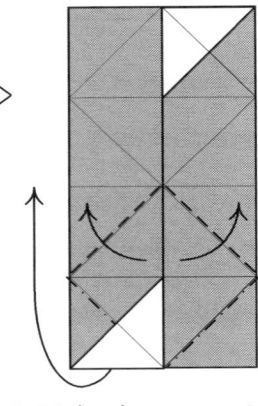

5. Make the mountain and valley folds while bringing bottom edge to center.

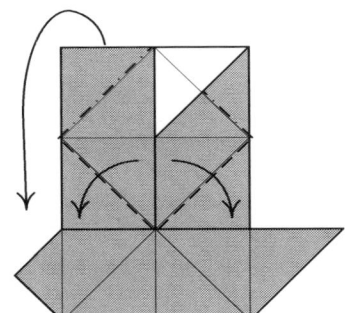

6. Repeat Step 5 on the top, bringing top edge to center.

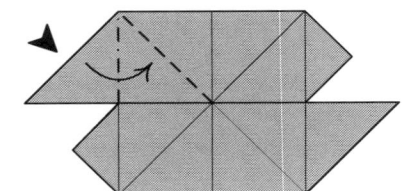

7. Squash corner.

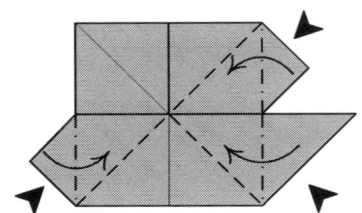

8. Repeat on other three corners.

Exquisite Modular Origami II

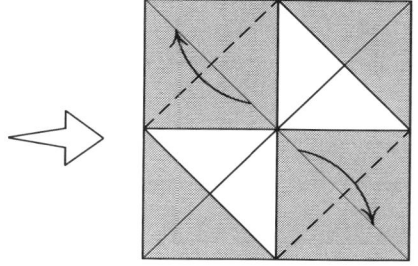

9. Valley fold two corners outwards.

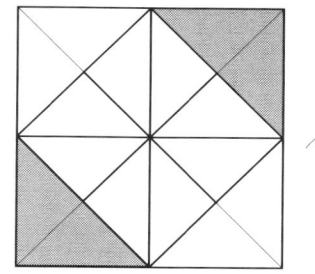

10. Turn over.

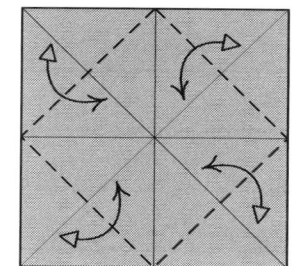

11. Blintz and unfold through all layers.

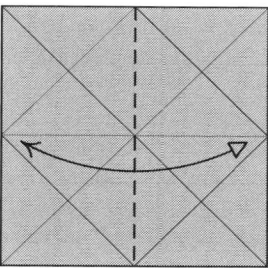

12. Valley fold and unfold through all layers.

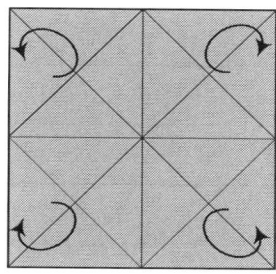

13. Tightly curl all corners towards you.

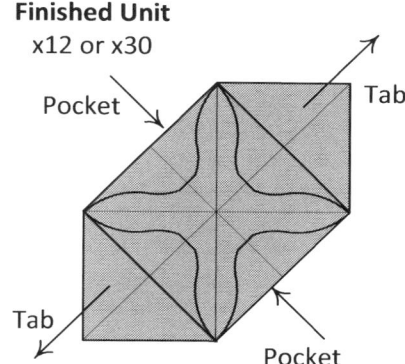

Finished Unit x12 or x30

Locking two units.

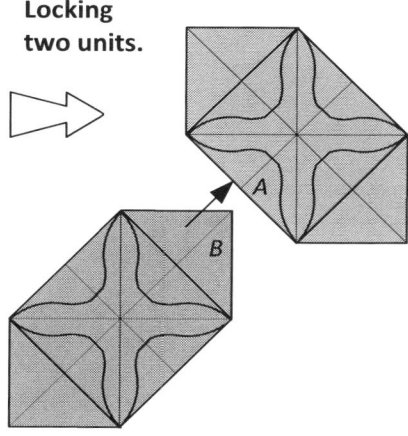

Uncurl pocket (A) of one unit to insert tab (B) of another unit into it. Re-curl together to secure the locking.

12 Unit Assembly

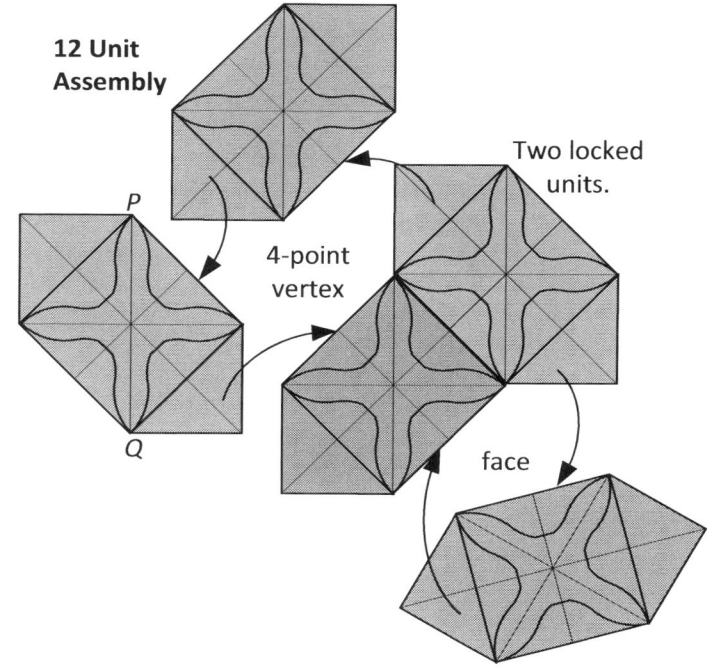

Exquisite Modular Origami II

For a **12-unit assembly** construct like an octahedron. Assemble 4 units in a ring to form a 4-point vertex. Add a fifth unit to form a triangular pyramid, the base of which will be a face of the octahedron. Continue constructing in this manner keeping in mind that line *PQ* of each unit will lie along the edges of the octahedron being constructed.

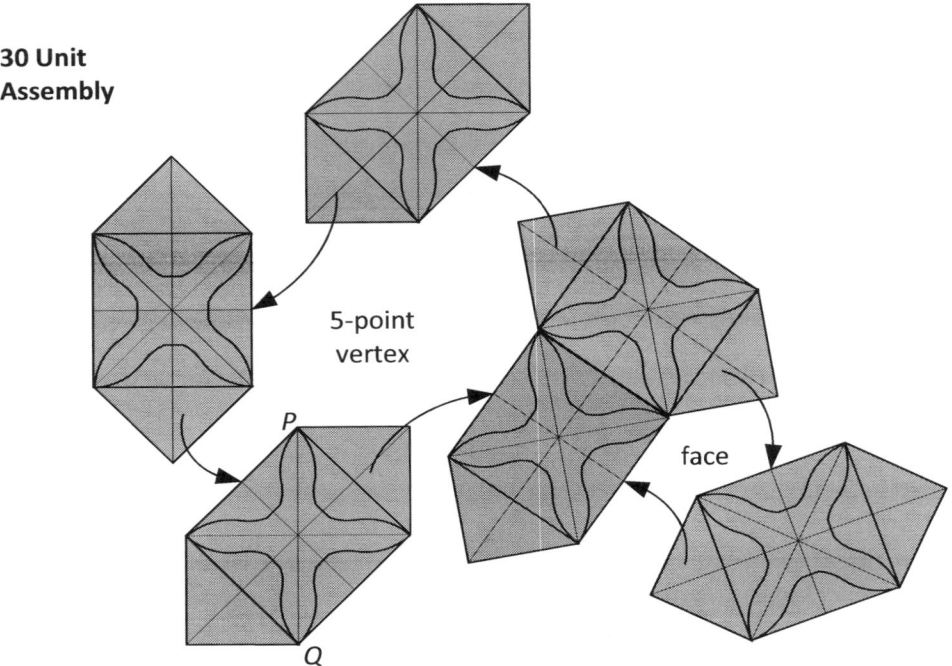

30 Unit Assembly

For a **30-unit assembly** construct like an icosahedron. Assemble 5 units in a ring to form a 5-point vertex. Add a sixth unit to form a triangular pyramid, the base of which will be a face of the icosahedron. Continue constructing in this manner keeping in mind that line *PQ* of each unit will lie along the edges of the icosahedron being constructed.

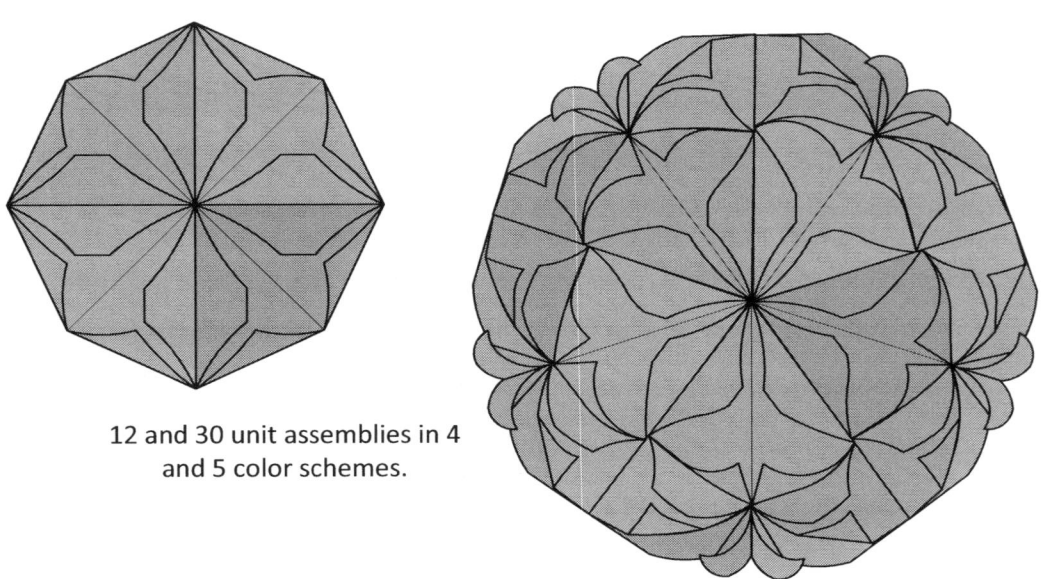

12 and 30 unit assemblies in 4 and 5 color schemes.

(Photo on cover, second row, left)

Zinnia 2 and Variation

(Created August 2011)

This is only a minor variation in the final folds to my original Zinnia design from 2007 (*Exquisite Modular Origami* [Muk11]), but the final result is quite different. For best results use Corona Harmony paper and size it to 2:3 proportion as explained on page 7.

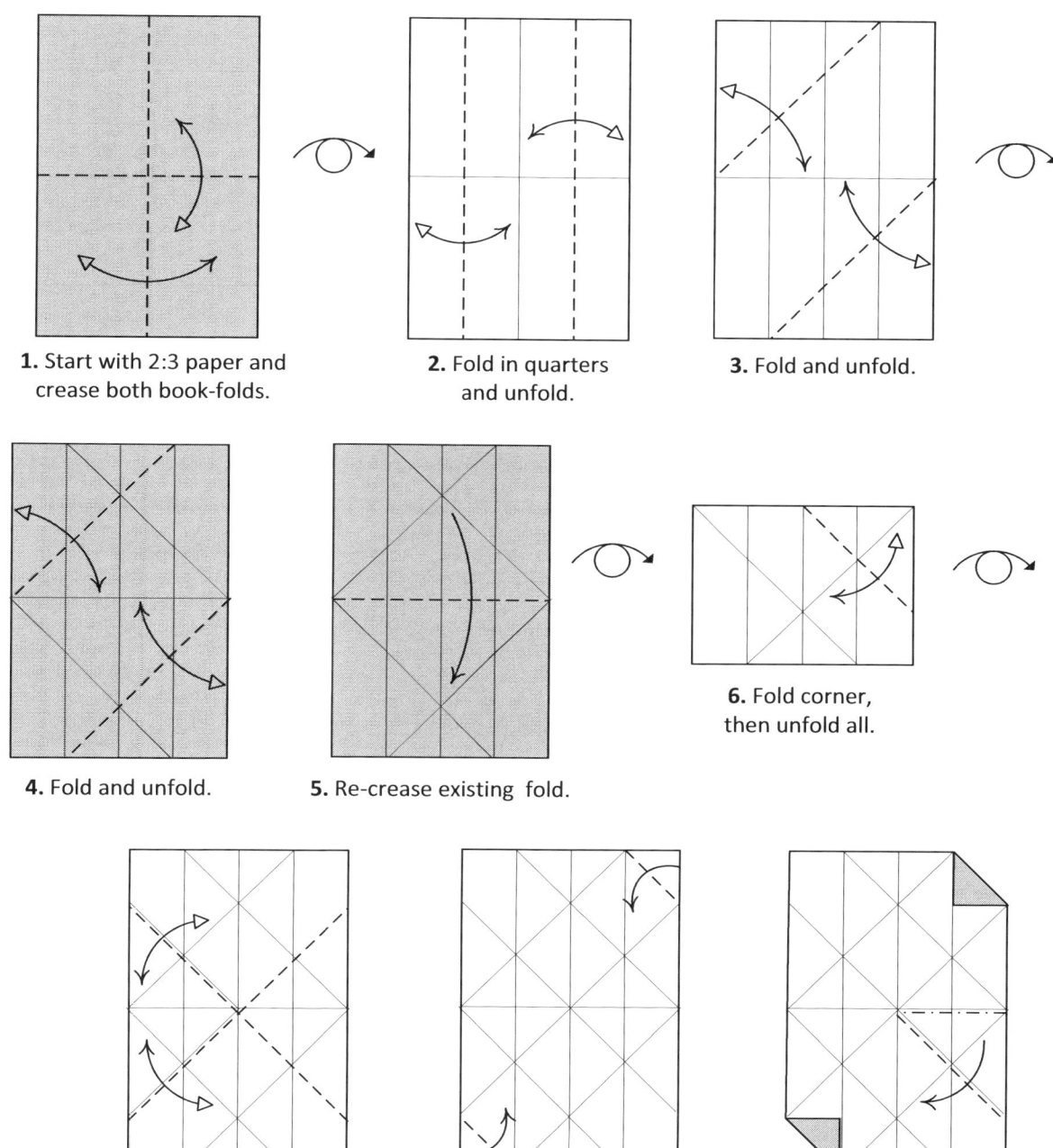

1. Start with 2:3 paper and crease both book-folds.

2. Fold in quarters and unfold.

3. Fold and unfold.

4. Fold and unfold.

5. Re-crease existing fold.

6. Fold corner, then unfold all.

7. Extend the creases made in Step 6.

8. Fold corners shown.

9. Valley and mountain fold existing creases.

10. Valley and mountain fold following the sequence numbers. Step *1* involves two layers of paper.

11. Turn around.

12. Repeat Steps 9 and 10. You need to reach within to collapse.

13. Valley fold.

14. Reverse fold and tuck.

15. Fold flaps.

16. Fold flaps.

17. Unfold last two steps and turn over.

18. Lift the flap to point towards you.

19. Insert your thumbs in the openings shown and fold the diagonal firmly. Do not crease the flap, just gently curve outwards like petals.

Exquisite Modular Origami II

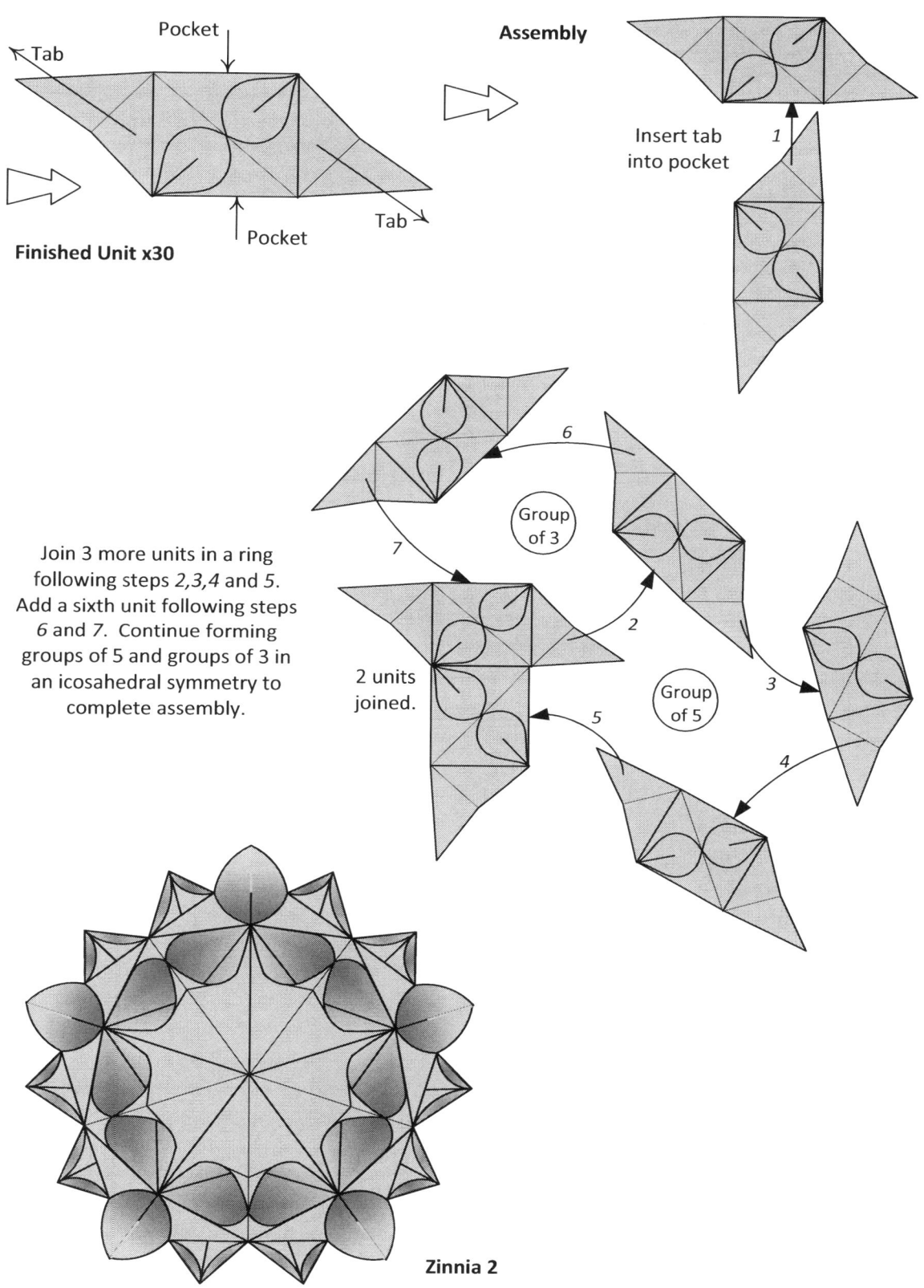

Finished Unit x30

Assembly

Insert tab into pocket

Join 3 more units in a ring following steps *2, 3, 4* and *5*. Add a sixth unit following steps *6* and *7*. Continue forming groups of 5 and groups of 3 in an icosahedral symmetry to complete assembly.

2 units joined.

Group of 3

Group of 5

Zinnia 2

(Photo on back cover, top row, second from left)

Color Change Variation of Zinnia 2

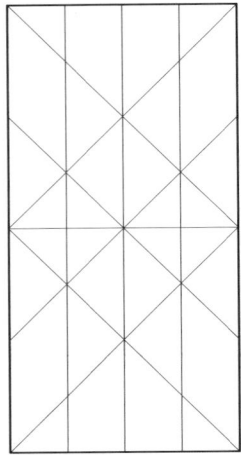

8'. Start with 1:2 paper and do Steps 1-7 of Zinnia 2.

9'. Fold the four corners.

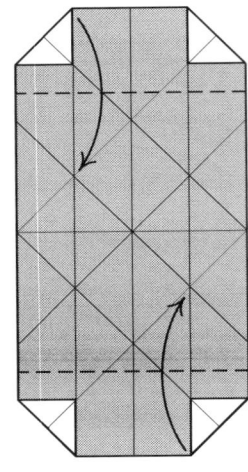

10'. Fold edges to reference points shown.

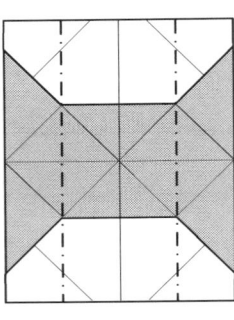

11'. Reinforce existing creases as mountain folds.

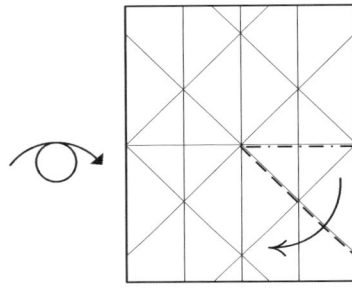

12'. Do Steps 9-12 of Zinnia 2 through all layers.

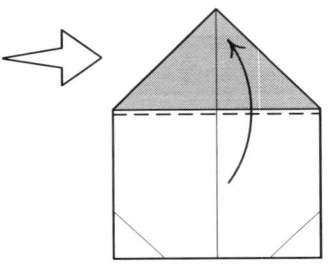

13'. Fold front flap up.

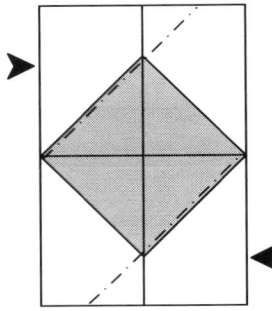

14'. Do Steps 14-19 of Zinnia 2 to complete unit. Note that the tabs will be blunt.

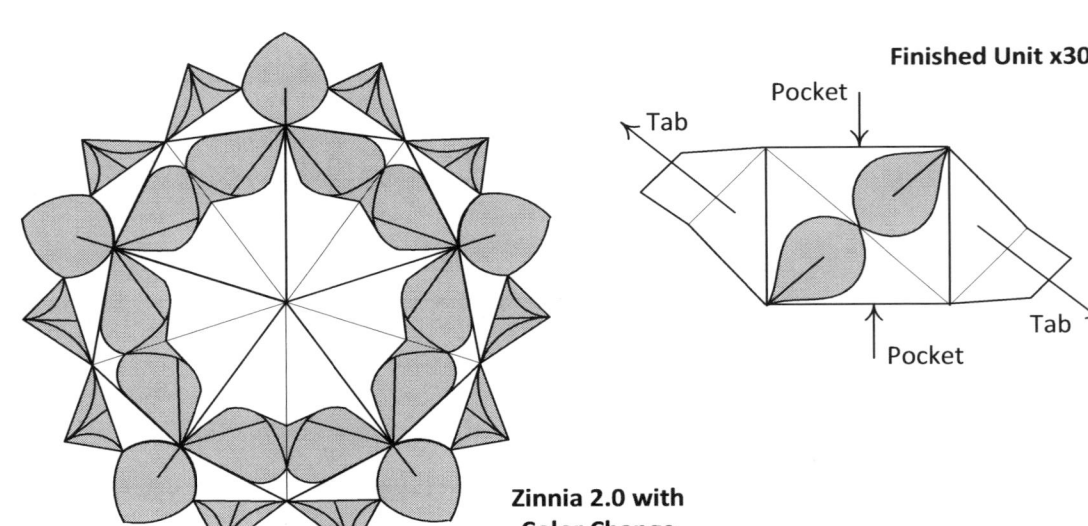

Zinnia 2.0 with Color Change

Finished Unit x30

Exquisite Modular Origami II

Curled Sonobe

(Created May 2012)

The Sonobe unit never ceases to amaze. Here is yet another minor variation with a pleasing finish. The unit has heavy similarities with the *Diabolo Unit* by Kunihiko Kasahara, which in turn borrows from other Sonobe type models by Tomoko Fuse. But my end-result is sufficiently different to make me want to diagram. So, in summary, this model is inspired by Mitsunobu Sonobe, Tomoko Fuse and Kunihiko Kasahara.

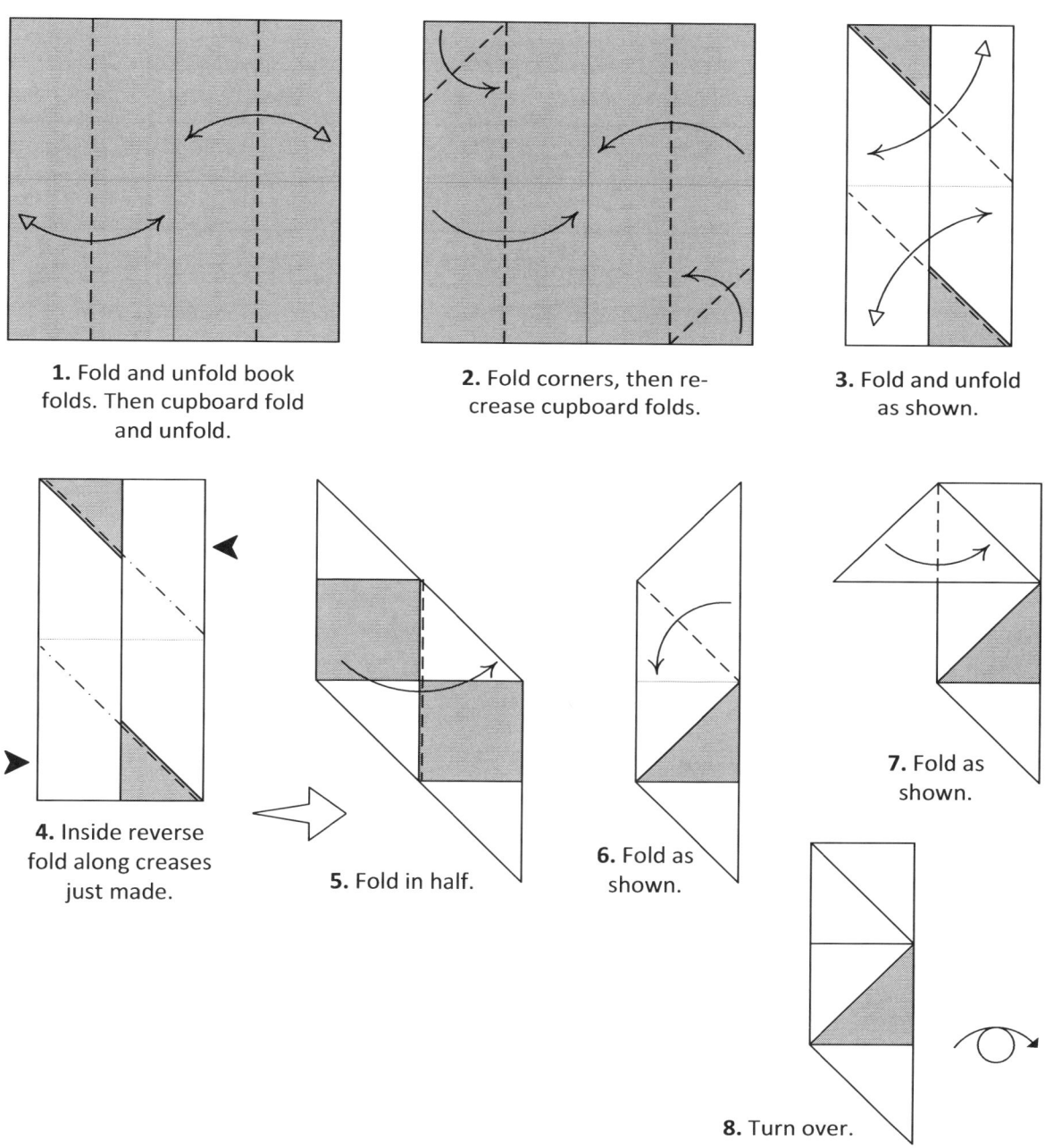

1. Fold and unfold book folds. Then cupboard fold and unfold.

2. Fold corners, then re-crease cupboard folds.

3. Fold and unfold as shown.

4. Inside reverse fold along creases just made.

5. Fold in half.

6. Fold as shown.

7. Fold as shown.

8. Turn over.

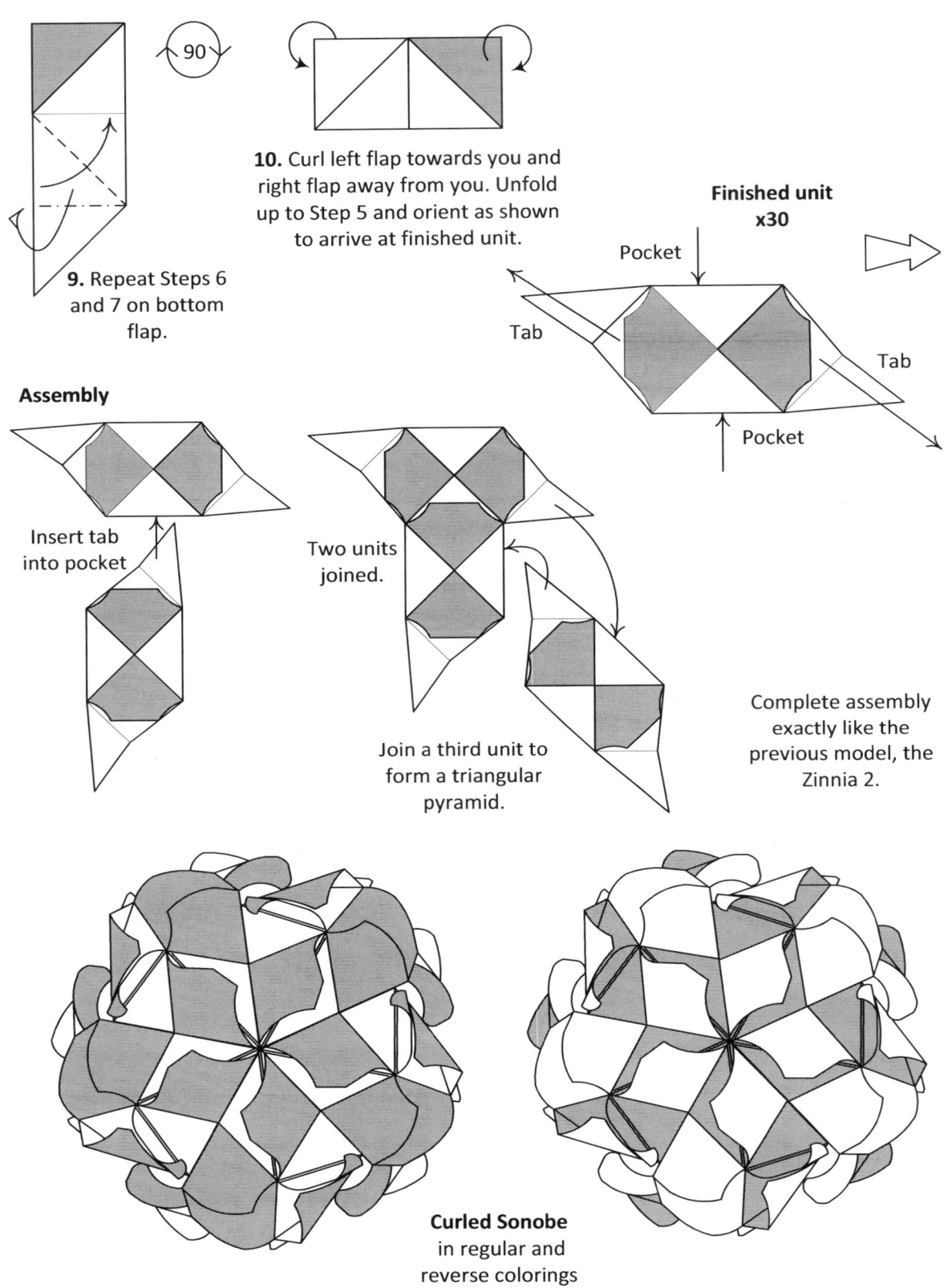

9. Repeat Steps 6 and 7 on bottom flap.

10. Curl left flap towards you and right flap away from you. Unfold up to Step 5 and orient as shown to arrive at finished unit.

Finished unit x30

Pocket / Tab / Tab / Pocket

Assembly

Insert tab into pocket

Two units joined.

Join a third unit to form a triangular pyramid.

Complete assembly exactly like the previous model, the Zinnia 2.

Curled Sonobe in regular and reverse colorings

(Photo on Cover, second row, right)

Exquisite Modular Origami II

34

Juhi Sonobe

(Created June 2014)

Juhi is the Indian name for the Jasmine flower.

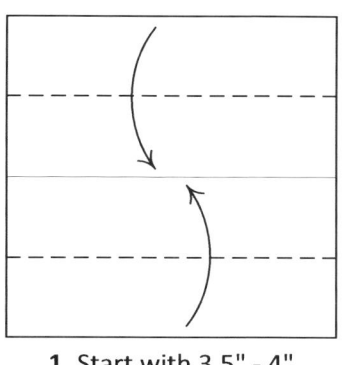

1. Start with 3.5" - 4" square. Crease in half, then fold quarters.

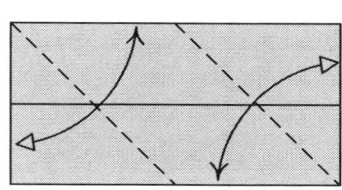

2. Fold corners and unfold.

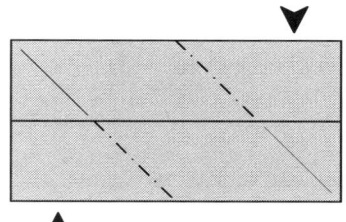

3. Reverse fold along creases just made.

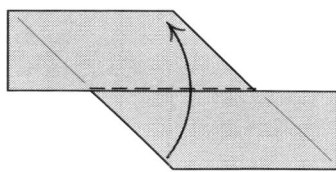

4. Fold in half.

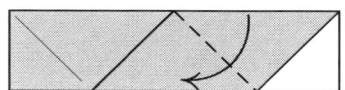

5. Fold right side.

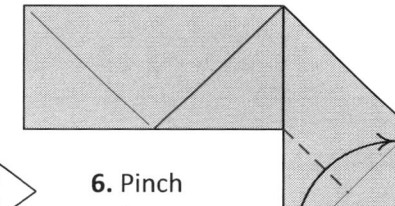

6. Pinch as shown.

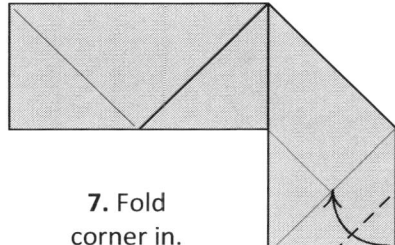

7. Fold corner in.

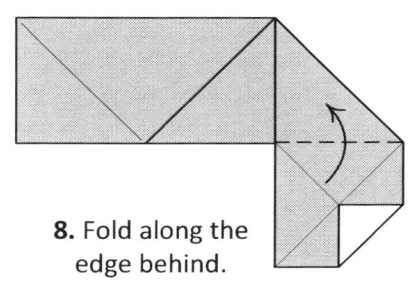

8. Fold along the edge behind.

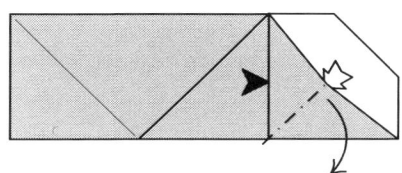

9. Squash without creasing the white part.

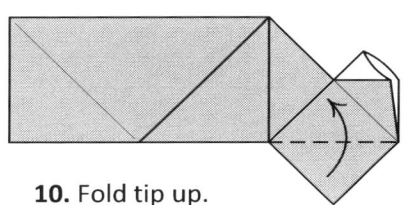

10. Fold tip up.

Exquisite Modular Origami II

11. Turn over and repeat Steps 5-10 on the other side.

Finished Unit x30
Unfold slightly.

Assembly

Join 2 units by inserting tab into pocket. The petals will meet.

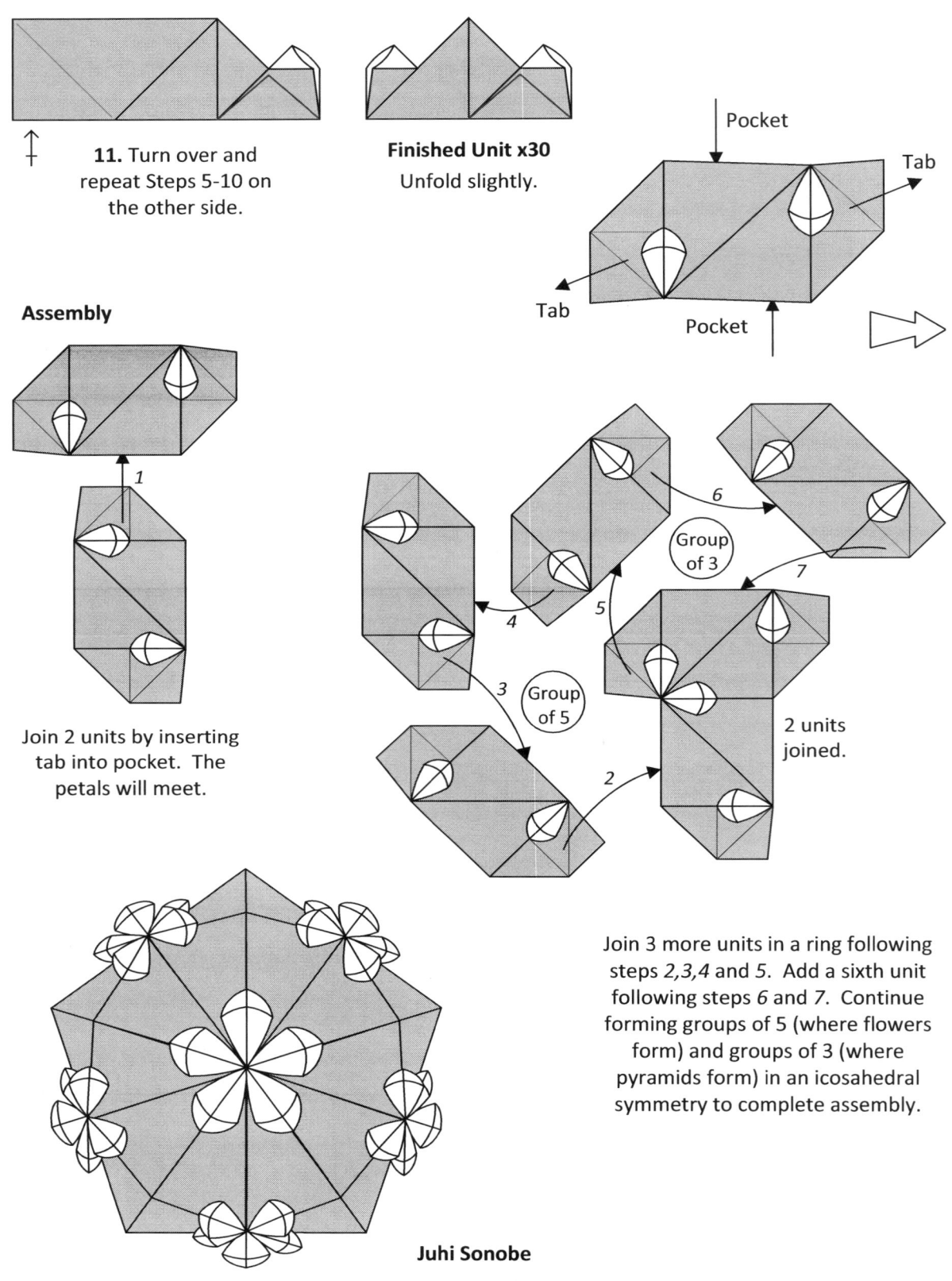

2 units joined.

Join 3 more units in a ring following steps *2,3,4* and *5*. Add a sixth unit following steps *6* and *7*. Continue forming groups of 5 (where flowers form) and groups of 3 (where pyramids form) in an icosahedral symmetry to complete assembly.

Juhi Sonobe

(Photo on back cover bottom left)

Exquisite Modular Origami II

Centaury
(Created May 2014)

Obtain the starting paper size of 3"x5.5" rectangles as explained on page 7.

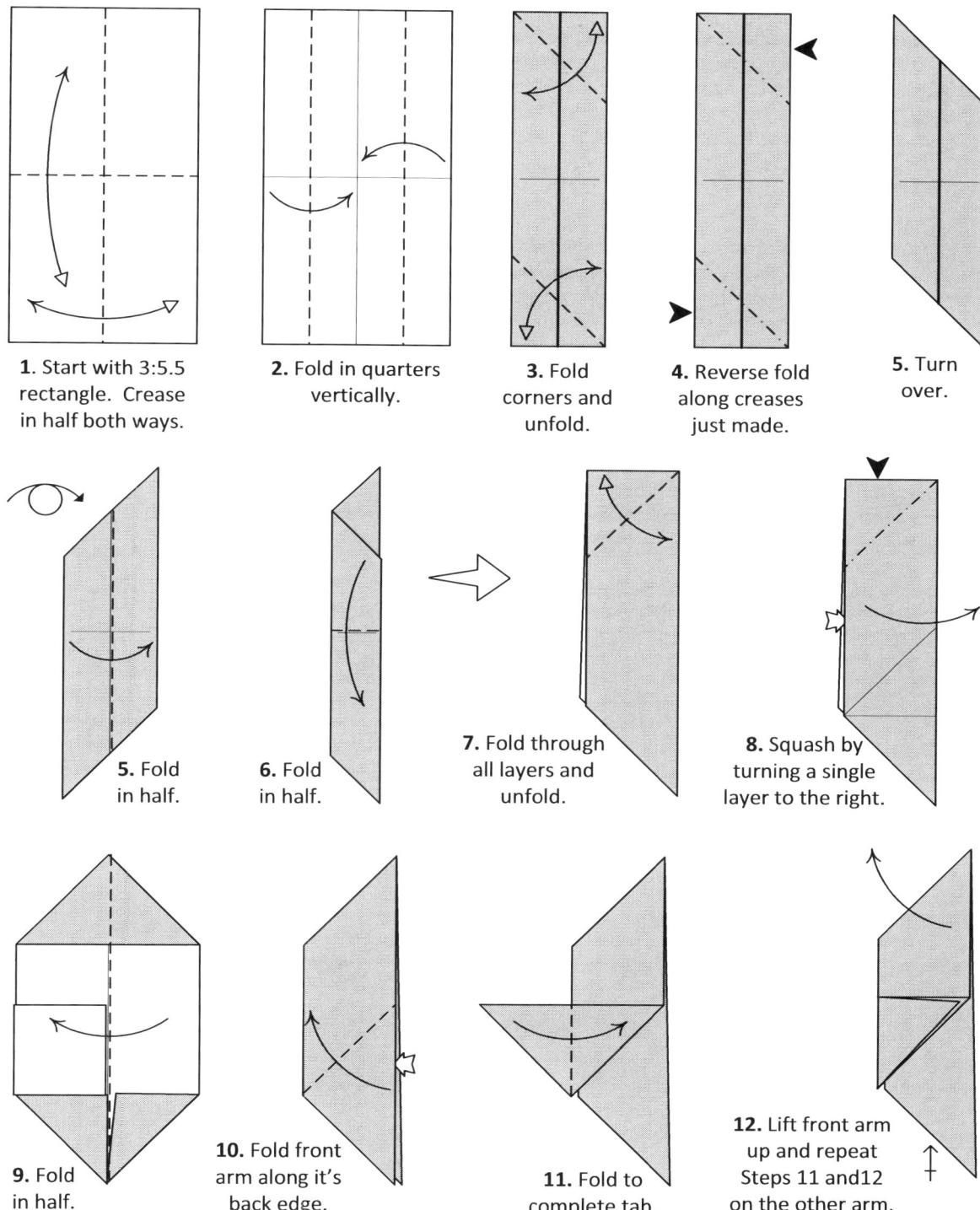

13. Spread open petals and curve outwards to shape.

Finished Unit x30
(Top View)

Tab

Pocket

Pocket

Tab

Assembly

Join 2 units by inserting tab into pocket.

2 units joined.

Group of 5

Group of 3

Join 3 more units in a ring following steps *2,3,4* and *5*. Add a sixth unit following steps *6* and *7*. Continue forming groups of 5 (where the flowers form) and groups of 3 (where the holes form) in an icosahedral symmetry to complete assembly.

Centaury

(Photo on back cover, top row, right)

Exquisite Modular Origami II

Columbine

(Created May 2014)

Obtain the starting paper size of 3"x5.5" rectangles as explained on page 7.

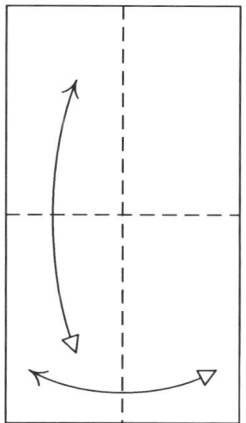 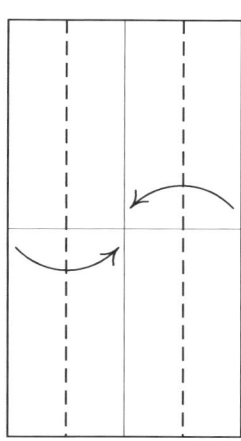 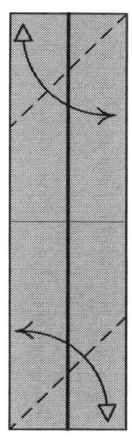 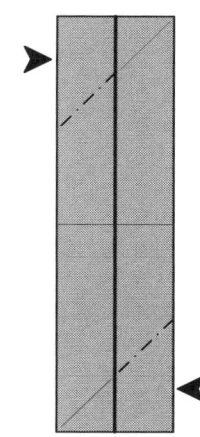 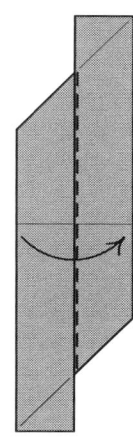

1. Start with 3:5.5 rectangle. Crease in half both ways.

2. Fold in quarters vertically.

3. Fold corners and unfold.

4. Reverse fold along creases just made.

5. Fold vertically in half.

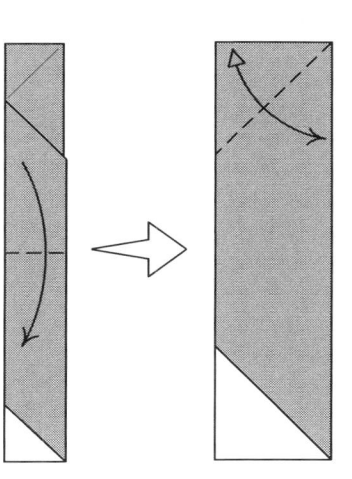 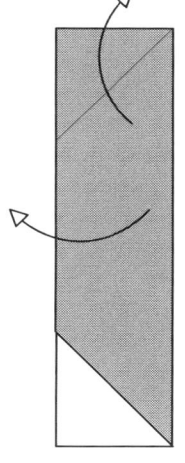 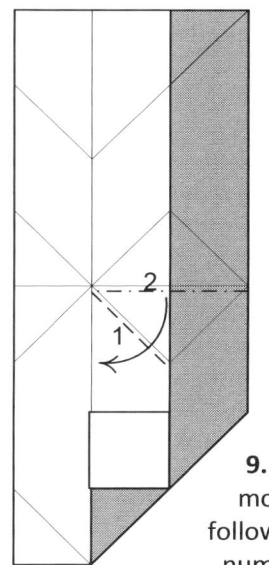

6. Fold in half.

7. Fold corner through all layers and unfold.

8. Unfold several steps so it is like next step.

9. Valley and mountain fold following sequence numbers. Do not flatten the unit.

Exquisite Modular Origami II

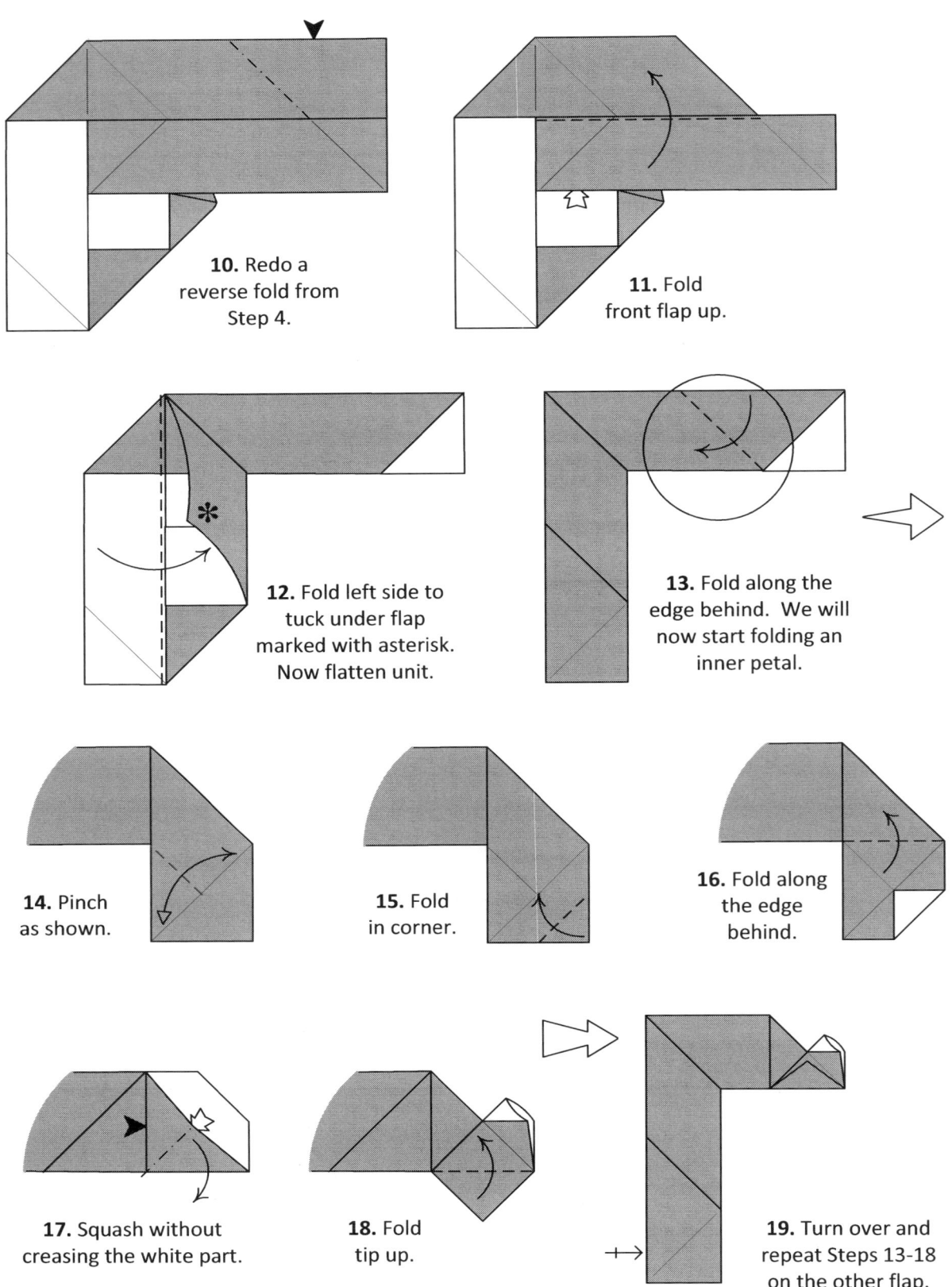

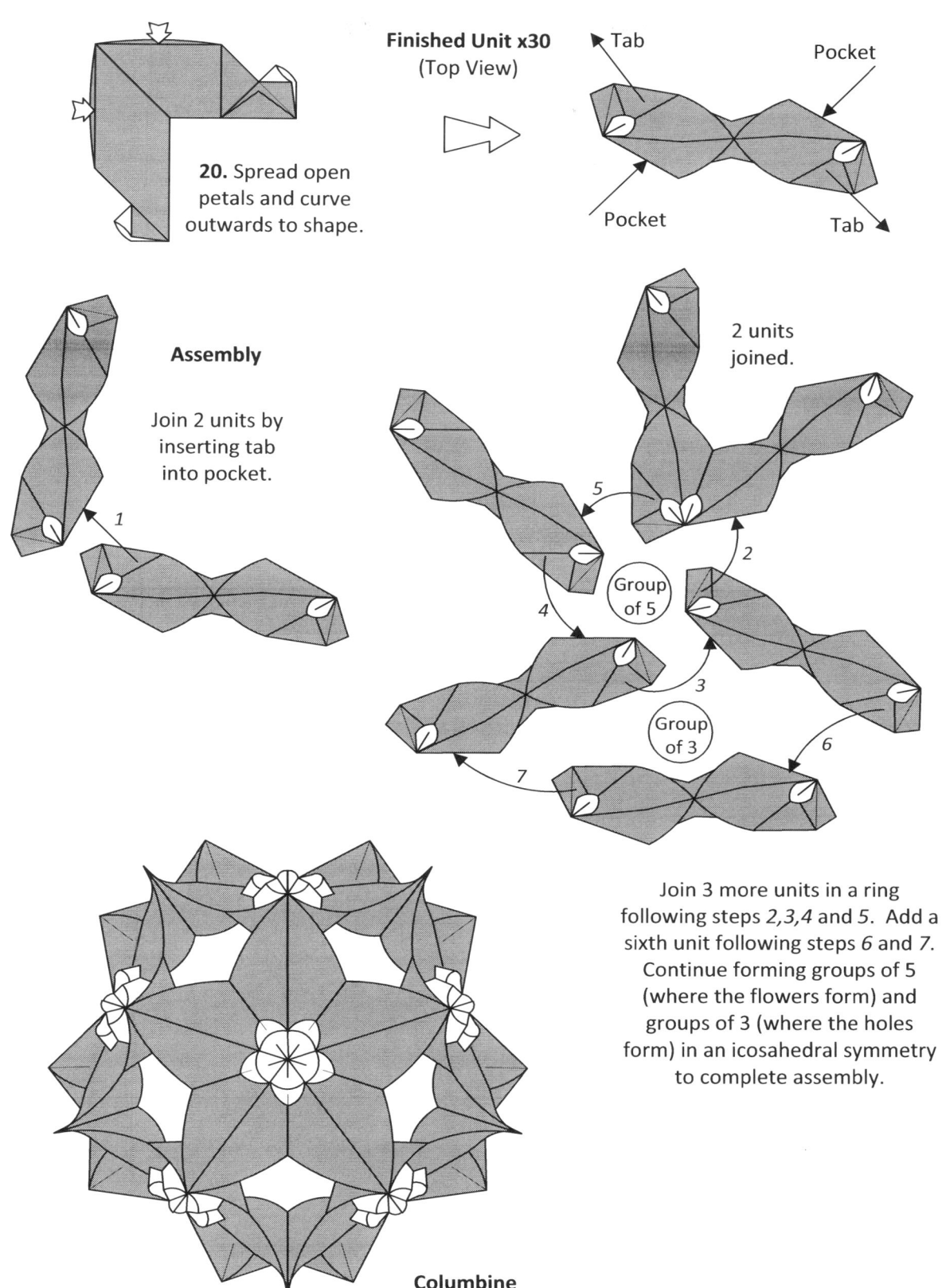

20. Spread open petals and curve outwards to shape.

Finished Unit x30 (Top View) — Tab, Pocket, Pocket, Tab

Assembly

Join 2 units by inserting tab into pocket.

2 units joined.

Group of 5

Group of 3

Join 3 more units in a ring following steps *2*, *3*, *4* and *5*. Add a sixth unit following steps *6* and *7*. Continue forming groups of 5 (where the flowers form) and groups of 3 (where the holes form) in an icosahedral symmetry to complete assembly.

Columbine

(Photo on cover, second row, middle)

Exquisite Modular Origami II

Gerbera and Variations

(Created June 2014)

Obtain the starting paper size of 3"x5.5" rectangles as explained on page 7.

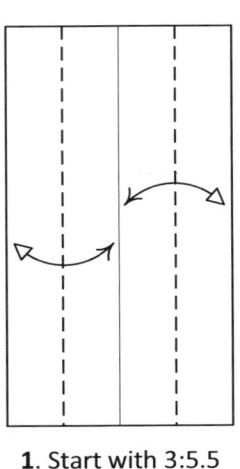

1. Start with 3:5.5 rectangle. Crease half and quarters.

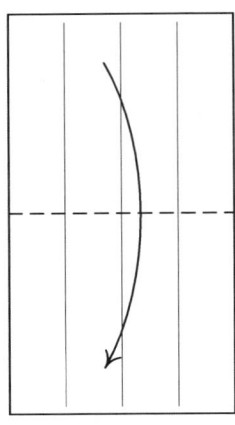

2. Fold in half.

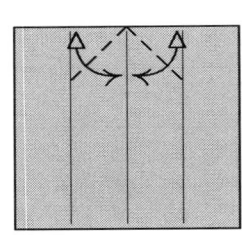

3. Fold only where shown. Unfold all.

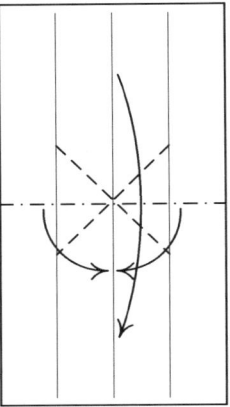

4. Collapse like a waterbomb base. Do not extend any creases or flatten.

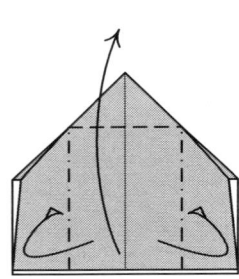

5. Lift front flap while folding as shown.

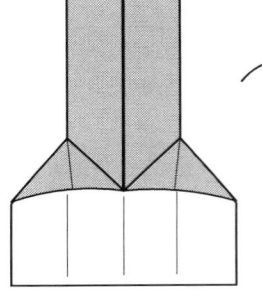

6. Turn over.

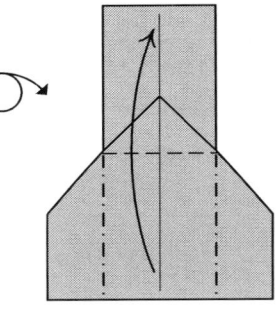

7. Repeat Step 5 and flatten.

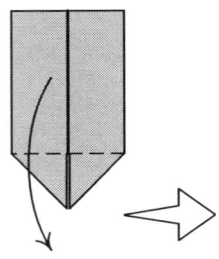

8. Fold front flap down.

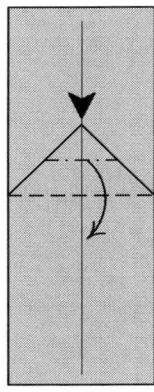

9. Lift tip and spread squash.

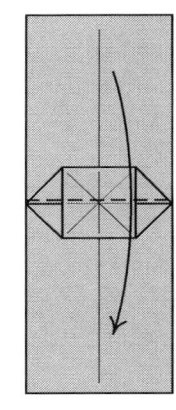

10. Fold flap down swiveling rear tips up.

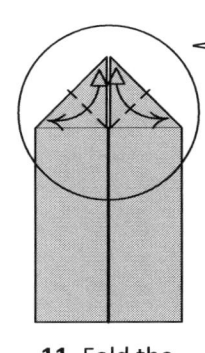

11. Fold the two tips and unfold.

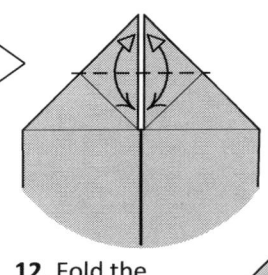

12. Fold the two tips and unfold.

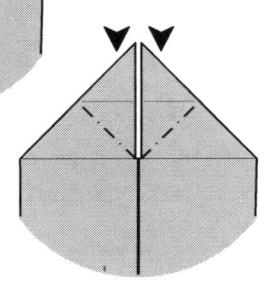

13. Reverse fold tips along creases from Step 11.

Exquisite Modular Origami II

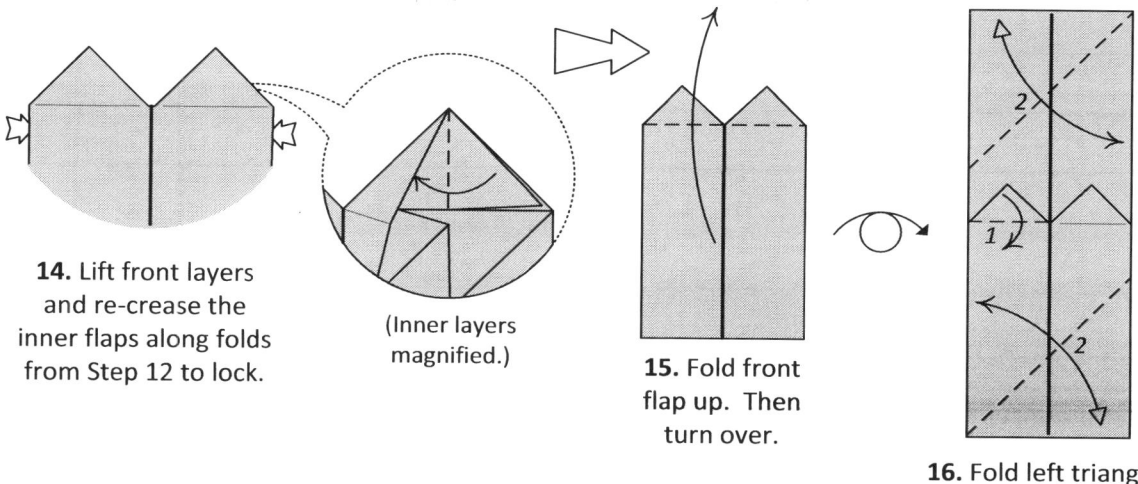

14. Lift front layers and re-crease the inner flaps along folds from Step 12 to lock.

(Inner layers magnified.)

15. Fold front flap up. Then turn over.

16. Fold left triangle down, then fold corners and unfold.

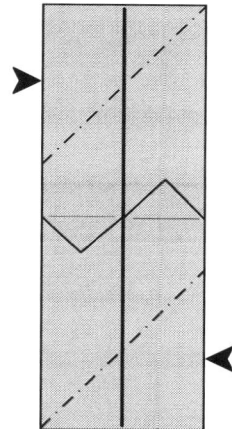
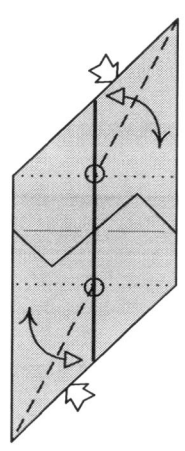
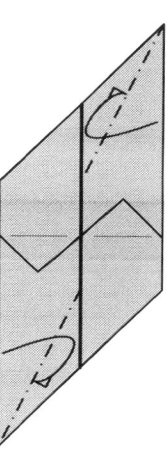
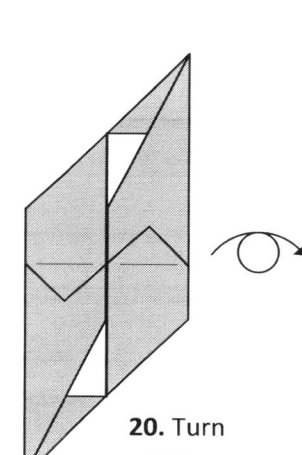

17. Reverse fold along creases just made.

18. Using hidden edges as reference fold front flaps and unfold.

19. Tuck along creases you just made.

20. Turn over.

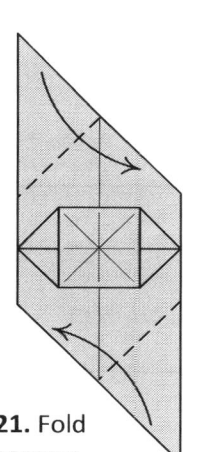
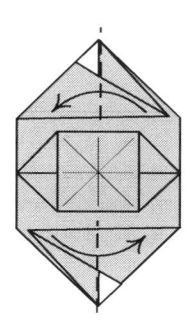
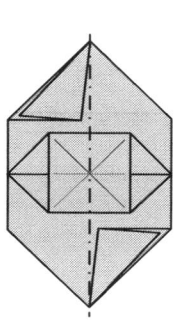
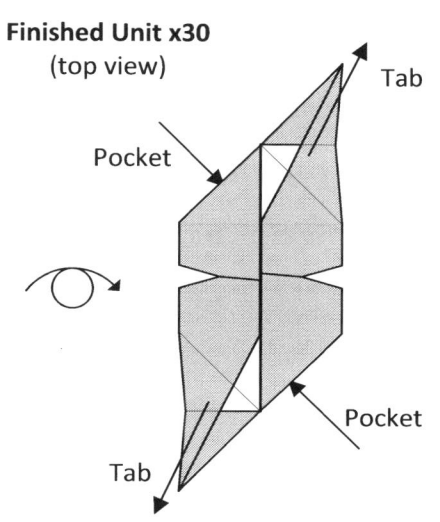

21. Fold corners.

22. Fold to complete tabs.

23. Mountain fold in half.

Finished Unit x30
(top view)

Tab
Pocket
Pocket
Tab

Exquisite Modular Origami II

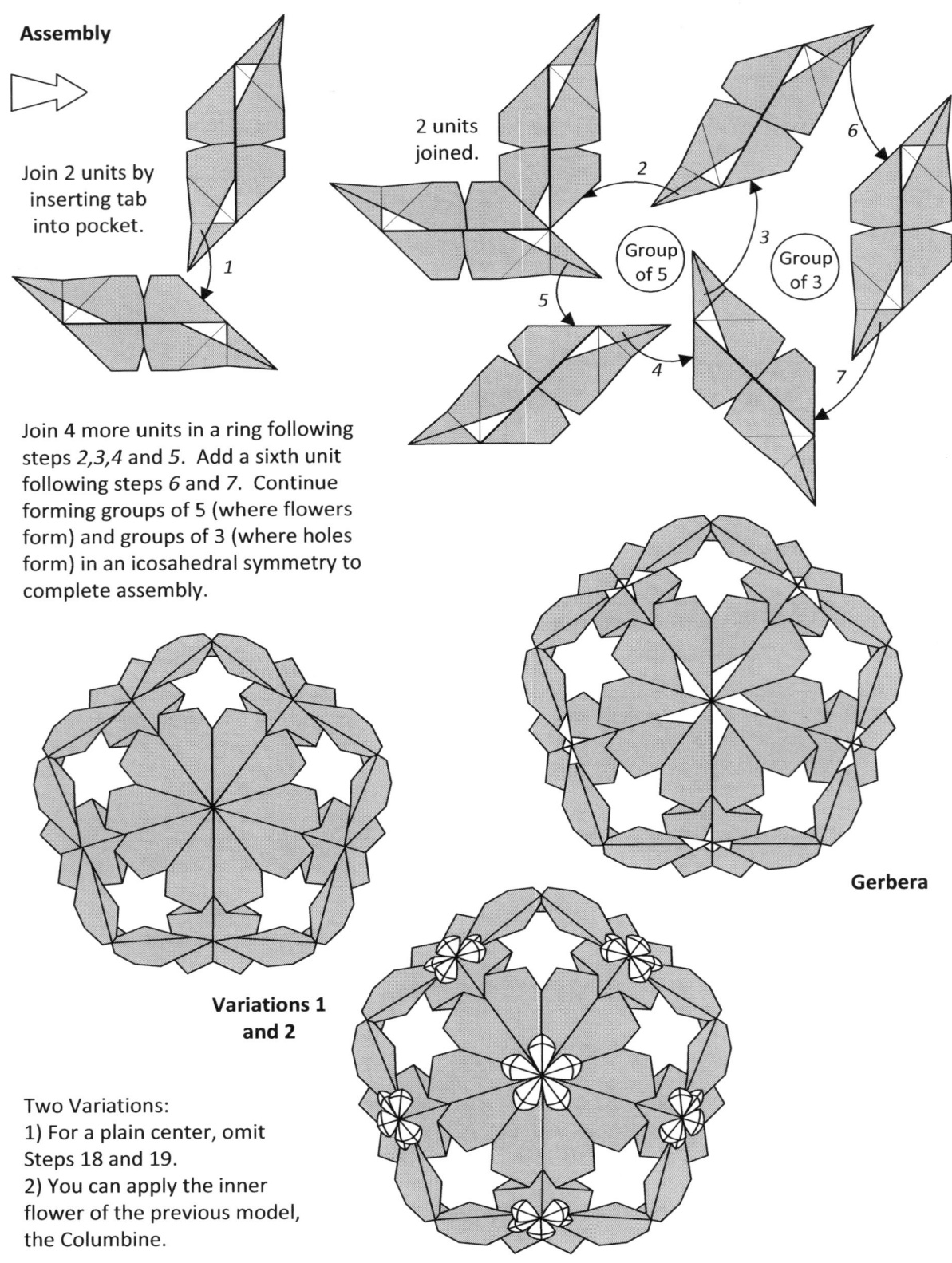

Assembly

Join 2 units by inserting tab into pocket.

Join 4 more units in a ring following steps *2,3,4* and *5*. Add a sixth unit following steps *6* and *7*. Continue forming groups of 5 (where flowers form) and groups of 3 (where holes form) in an icosahedral symmetry to complete assembly.

Variations 1 and 2

Two Variations:
1) For a plain center, omit Steps 18 and 19.
2) You can apply the inner flower of the previous model, the Columbine.

Gerbera

(Photo on cover, bottom row, right)

Poinsettia Floral Ball 2

(Created March 2012)

Note: This model is similar to my Poinsettia Floral Ball from 2003 (*Marvelous Modular Origami*, [Muk07]), but with slightly stronger locks.

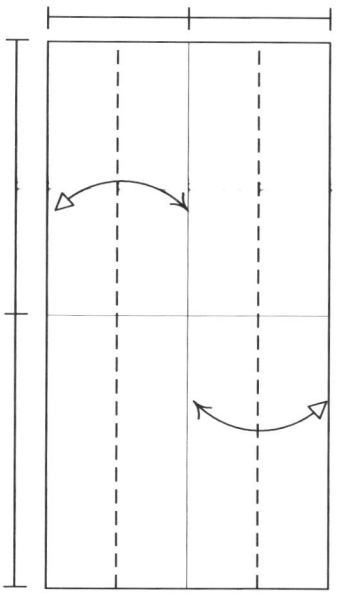

1. Start with 1:2 paper. Fold and unfold book-folds and cupboard folds.

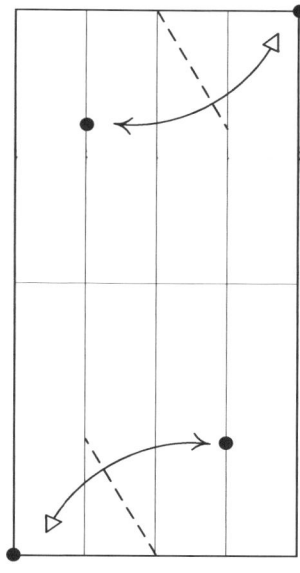

2. Match dots to form new creases as shown.

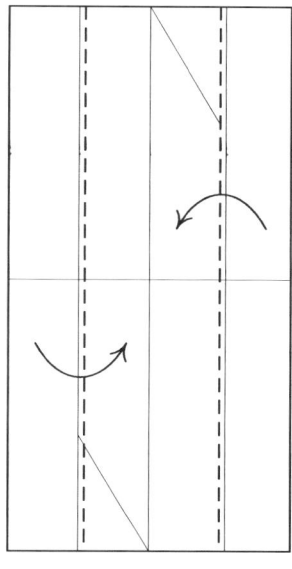

3. Re-crease cupboard folds

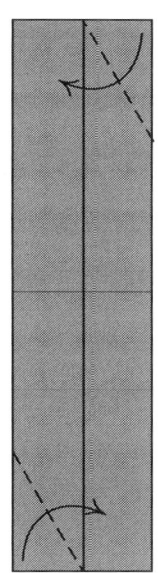

4. Fold and unfold to trace creases from Step 2 at the back.

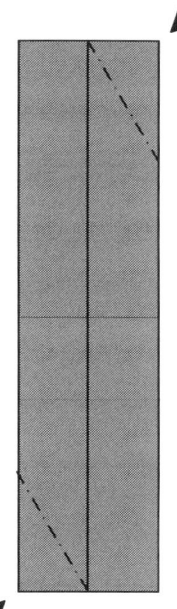

5. Reverse fold corners.

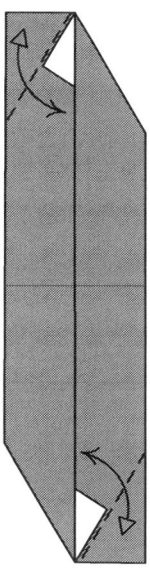

6. Fold and unfold along white edge.

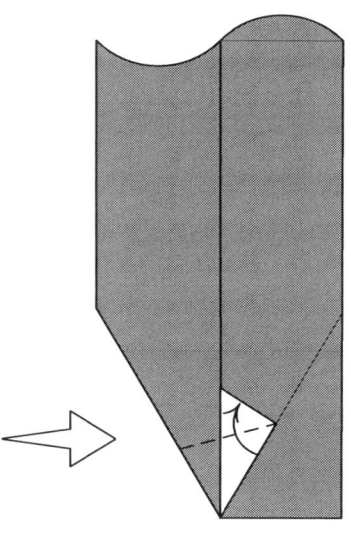

7. Fold to bisect angle as shown (showing bottom only).

Exquisite Modular Origami II

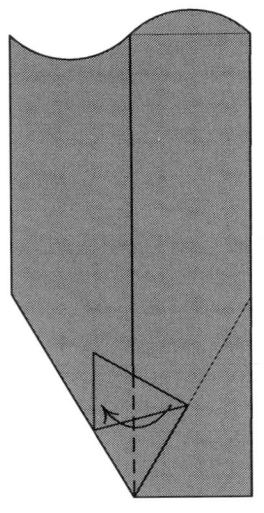

8. Fold flap to the left.

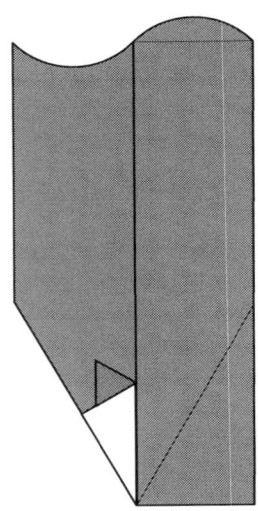

9. Repeat Steps 7 and 8 on top end.

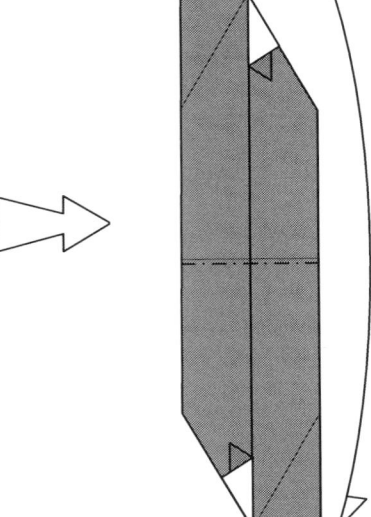

10. Mountain fold along existing crease.

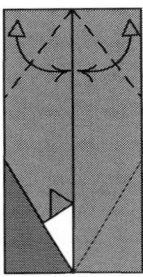

11. Fold and unfold corners.

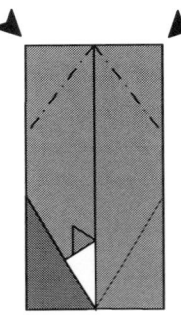

12. Reverse fold corners.

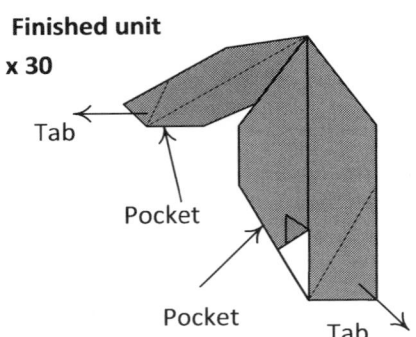

Finished unit x 30

Tab
Pocket
Pocket
Tab

Locking two units involves several steps as explained next.

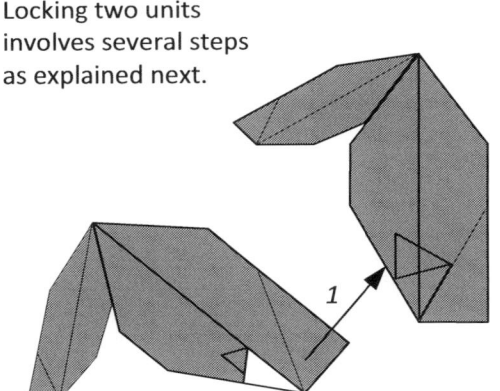

13. Undo Step 8 for the right hand unit. Insert tab of left unit into pocket of right unit.

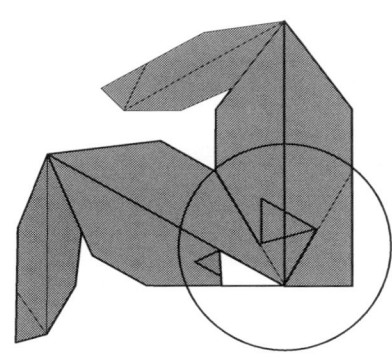

Exquisite Modular Origami II

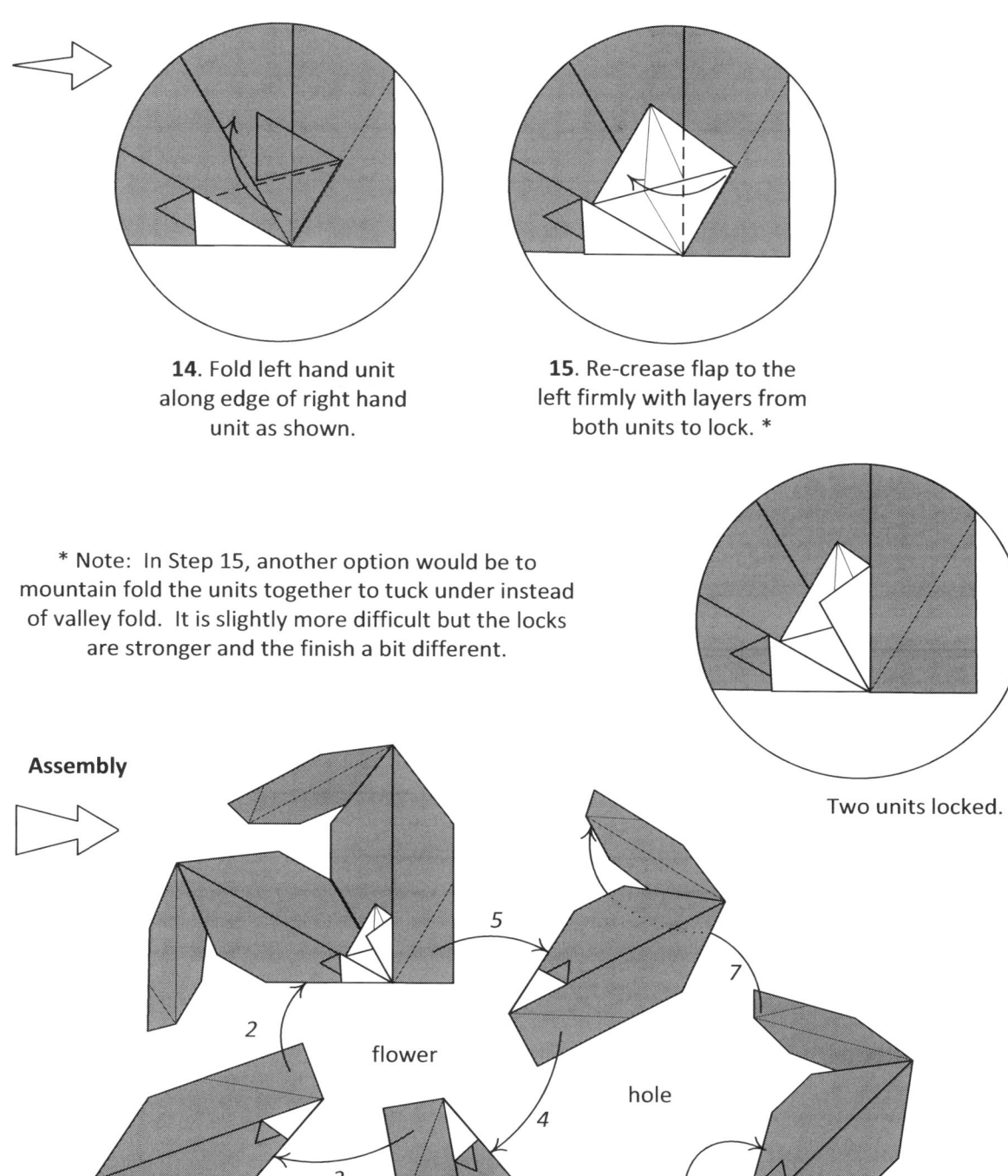

14. Fold left hand unit along edge of right hand unit as shown.

15. Re-crease flap to the left firmly with layers from both units to lock. *

* Note: In Step 15, another option would be to mountain fold the units together to tuck under instead of valley fold. It is slightly more difficult but the locks are stronger and the finish a bit different.

Two units locked.

Assembly

flower

hole

Assemble 5 units in a circle to form one flower, following sequence numbers *2-5*. Then insert a sixth unit following steps *6* and *7* to form one hole. Continue building 12 flowers and 20 holes to arrive at the finished model.

Exquisite Modular Origami II

Finished Poinsettia 2

Locking Variation:
Shows a bit more of the reverse color.

Do Steps 1-6 of Poinsettia 2.

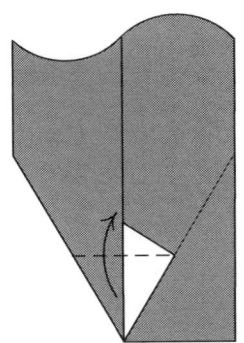

7'. Fold along line shown (showing bottom end only).

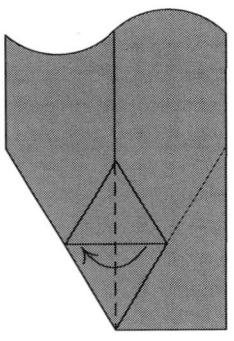 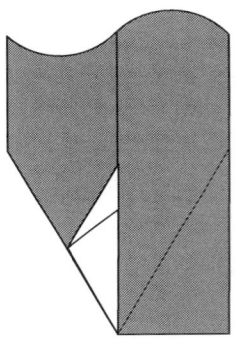

8'. Fold flap to the left.

9'. Repeat Steps 7' and 8' on top end.

Continue with Steps 10-12 of Poinsettia 2 and lock and assemble in the same way.

Finished Poinsettia 2 Variation.

Two units locked.

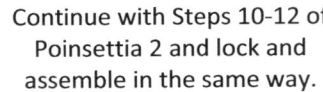

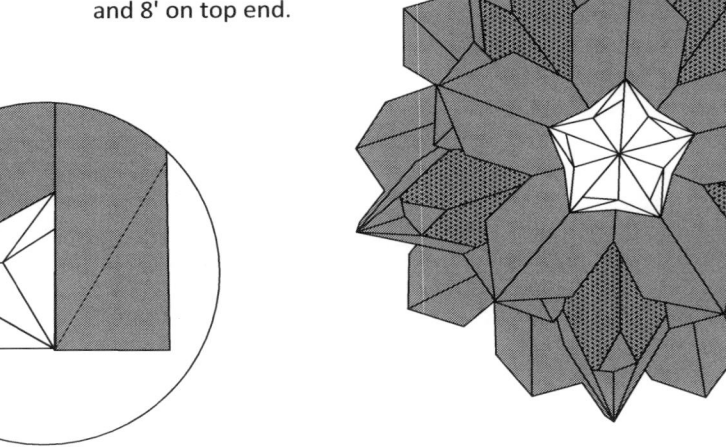

(Photo on back cover, top row, left)

Fanfare and Variation

(Created May 2014)

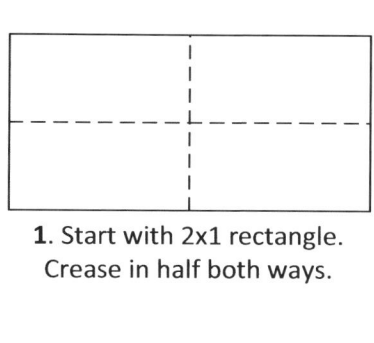

1. Start with 2x1 rectangle. Crease in half both ways.

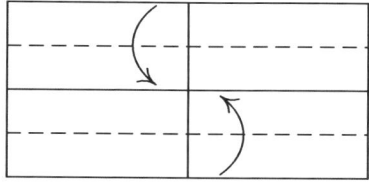

2. Fold into quarters.

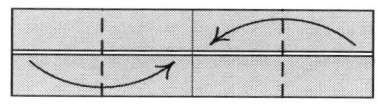

3. Fold into quarters and turn over.

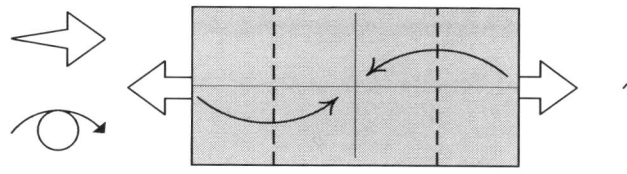

4. Fold while sliding rear flaps out. Turn over.

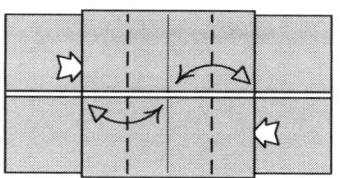

5. Fold top flap and unfold.

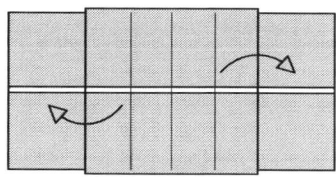

6. Unfold all the way back to Step 3.

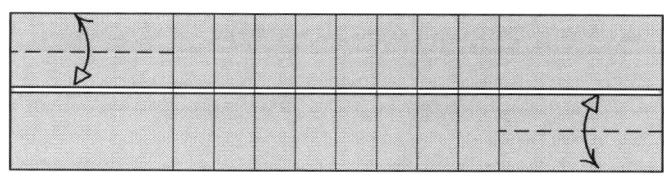

7. Fold halves where shown.

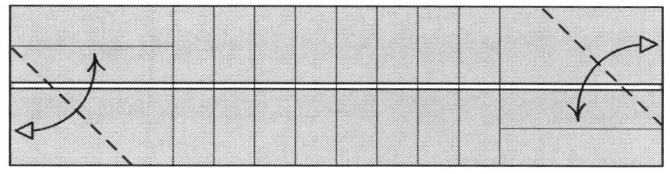

8. Fold edges to reference creases just made and unfold.

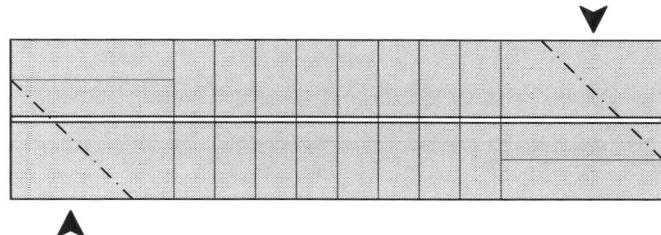

9. Reverse fold along the new creases.

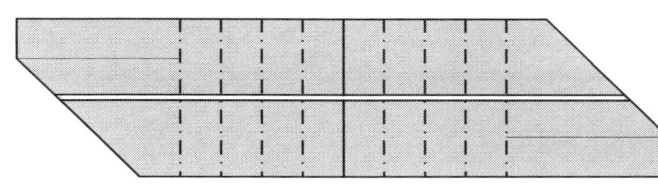

10. Reassign the 8 creases as mountain folds if they are not already so.

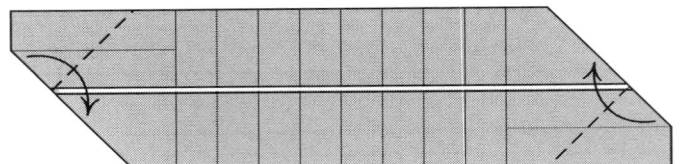

11. Fold the two ends.

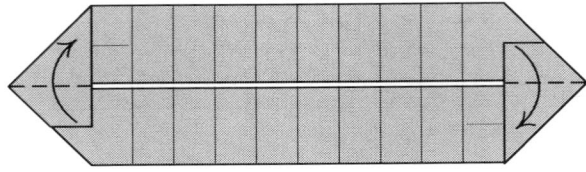

12. Fold as shown to complete the tabs.

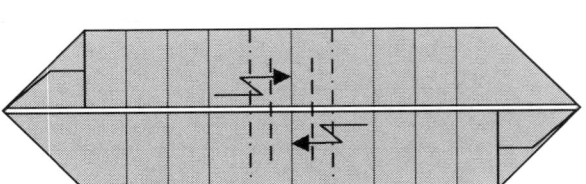

13. Pleat using existing mountain folds and making new partial valley folds. The new folds are creased at the center and only softly bent at the ends.

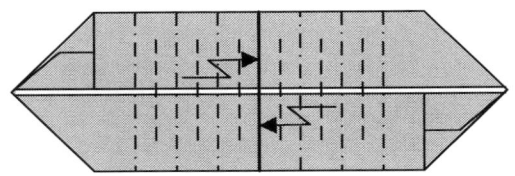

14. Similarly pleat the next set of creases, folding only the center and bending near the ends. Continue till you have 4 pleats on each side.

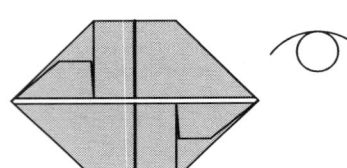

15. Turn over while holding all the pleats together.

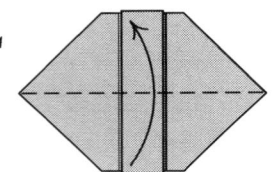

16. Fold through all layers, creasing firmly along the line. Do not flatten fan.

Finished Unit x30

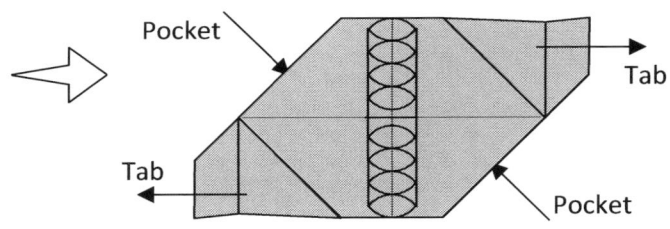

(If necessary, spread the two sections of the fan so they meet at the center.)

Assembly

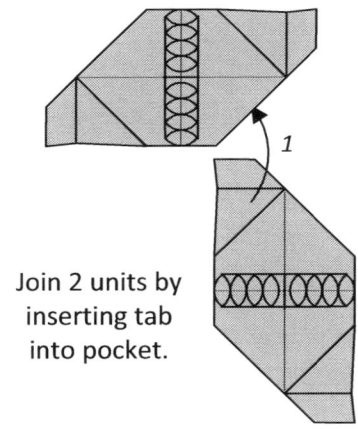

Join 2 units by inserting tab into pocket.

Exquisite Modular Origami II

50

Join 4 more units in a ring following steps *2,3,4* and *5*. Add a sixth unit following steps *6* and *7*. Continue forming groups of 5 and groups of 3 (where holes form) in an icosahedral symmetry to complete assembly. Note: You can also assemble 12 units in an octahedral symmetry.

Fanfare and its color change variation.

Note: The original design is best folded with Corona Harmony paper for accentuating the fans. You can also try the color change variation as shown next.

Color Change Variation

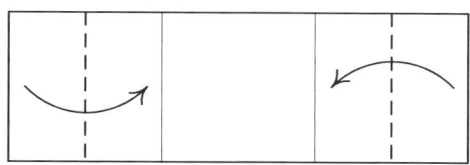

1. Start with 3"x9" paper and crease into thirds. Fold edges to third folds.

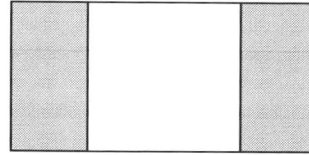

2. Turn over.

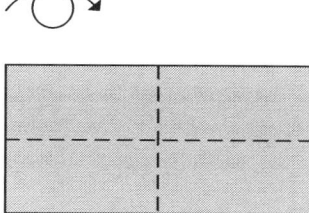

3. Fold all steps of the original Fanfare.

(Photo on page iii. Variation photo on cover, bottom row, middle)

Exquisite Modular Origami II

Origami My Heart

(Created April 2014)

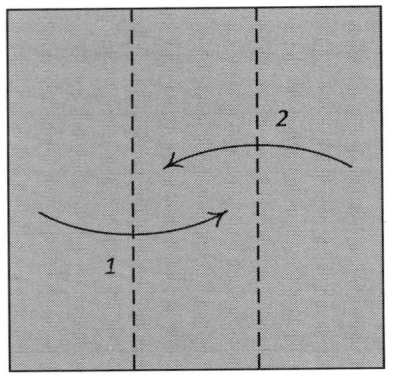

1. Fold into thirds.

2. Fold top layer only.

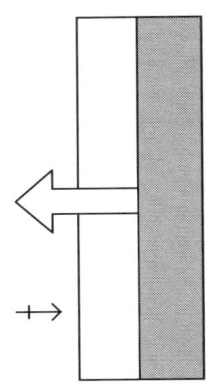

3. Pull left flap out and repeat.

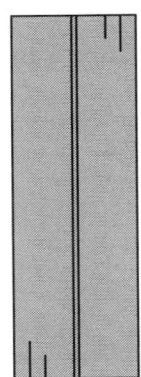

4. Pinch half and quarter points of the front flaps.

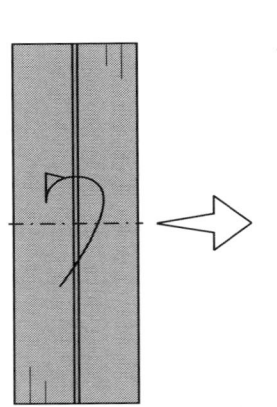

5. Mountain fold in half.

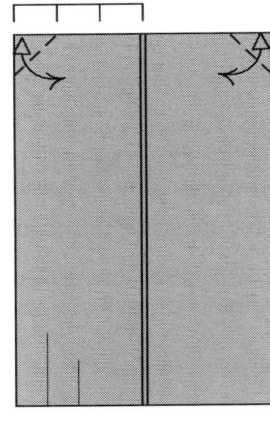

6. Fold the 2 corners at about 1/3 points. Unfold.

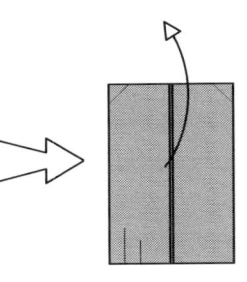

7. Unfold back to Step 5.

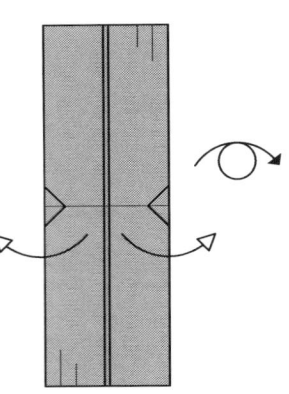

8. Unfold the original 1/3 creases shown.

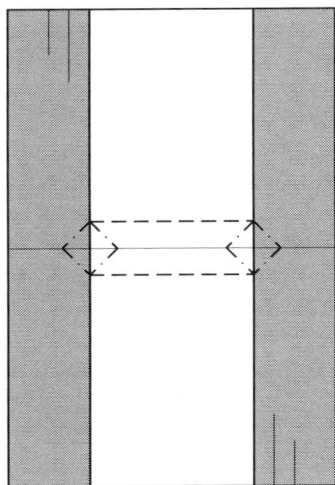

9. Reinforce the diamonds as mountain folds. Make the 2 new valley folds.

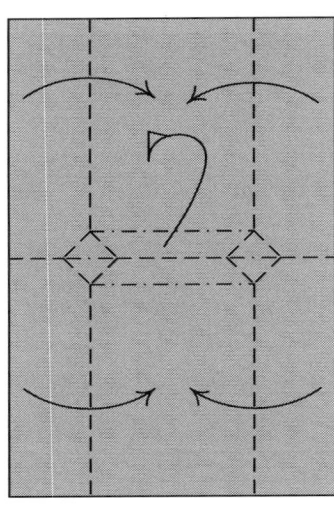

10. Collapse following gender of the creases to arrive at the next step.

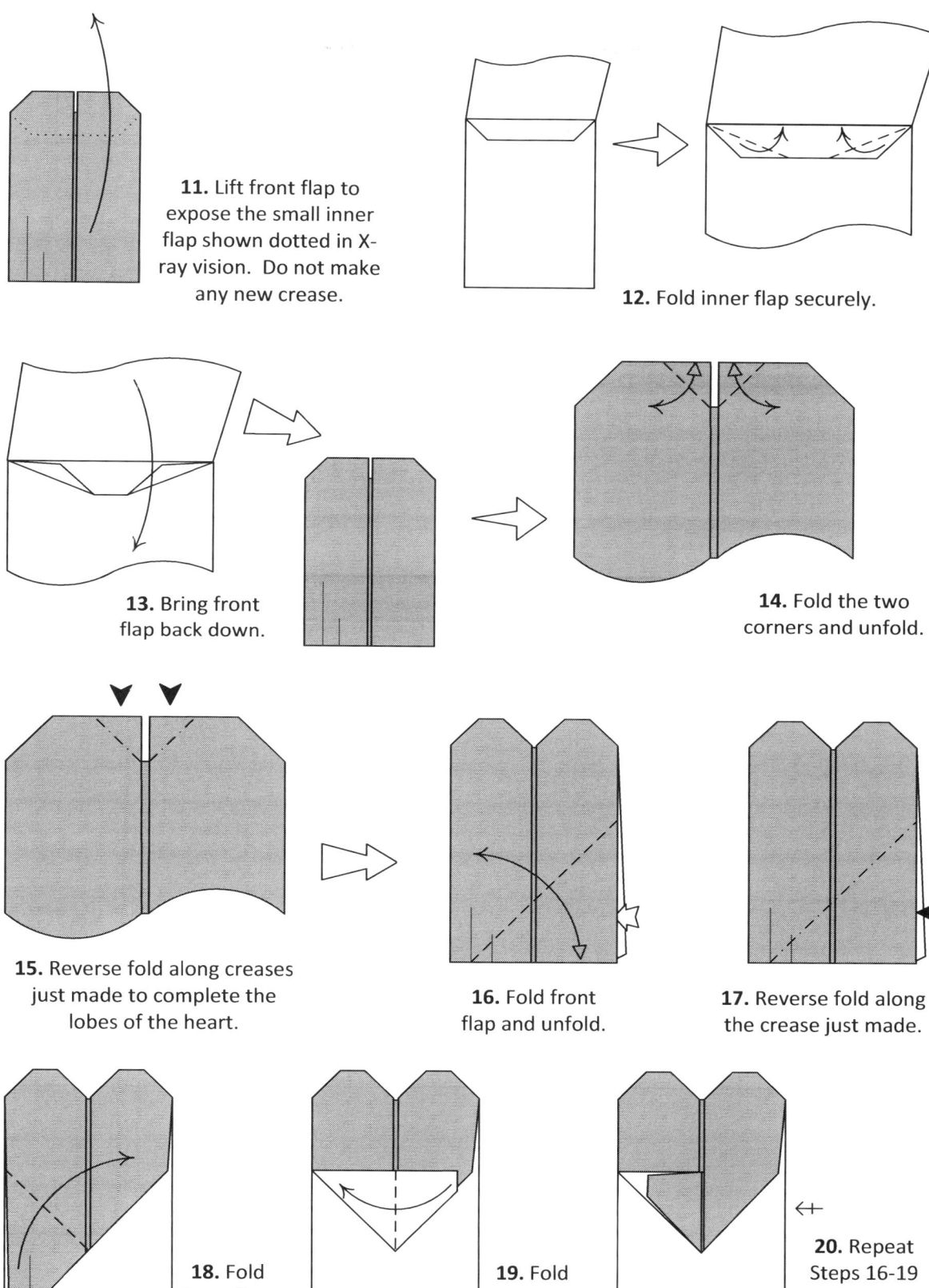

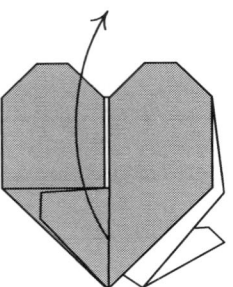

21. Lift the front heart without creasing lobes.

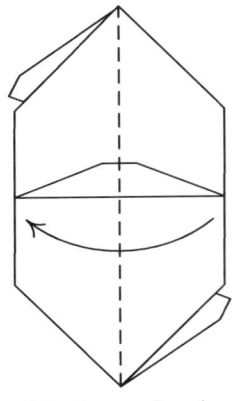

22. Crease firmly through all layers. Make sure that the middle flap is oriented with its plain side visible.

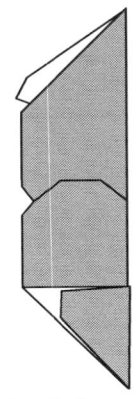

23. Lobes should be perpendicular to unit. Unfold unit slightly.

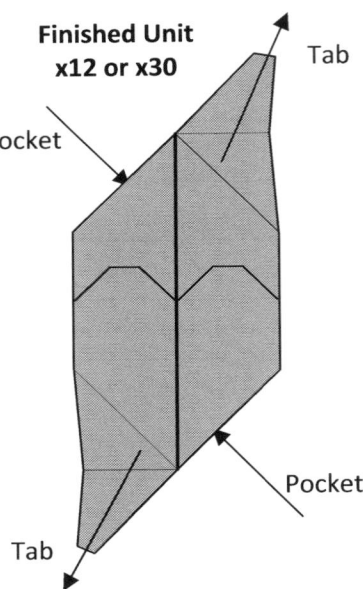

Finished Unit x12 or x30

Tab
Pocket
Pocket
Tab

12-unit Assembly

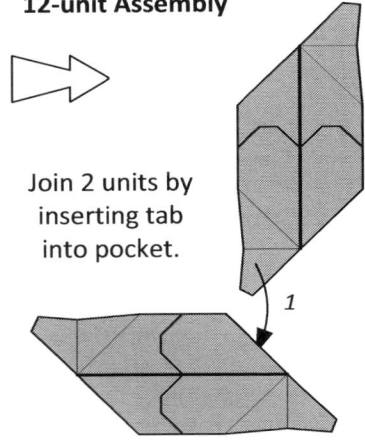

Join 2 units by inserting tab into pocket.

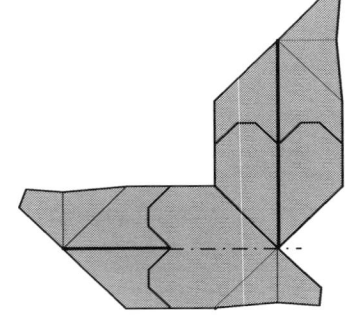

Reinforce the mountain fold through layers of both units to lock securely. You may need to repeat this several times during the assembly process.

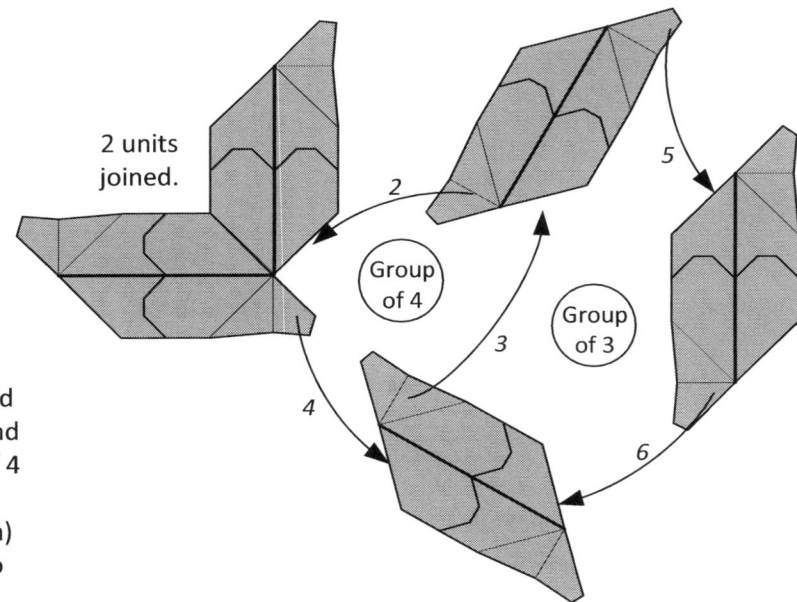

2 units joined.

Group of 4

Group of 3

Join 2 more units in a ring following steps *2,3*, and *4*. Add a fifth unit following steps *5* and *6*. Continue forming groups of 4 (where flowers form) and groups of 3 (where holes form) in an octahedral symmetry to complete assembly.

Exquisite Modular Origami II

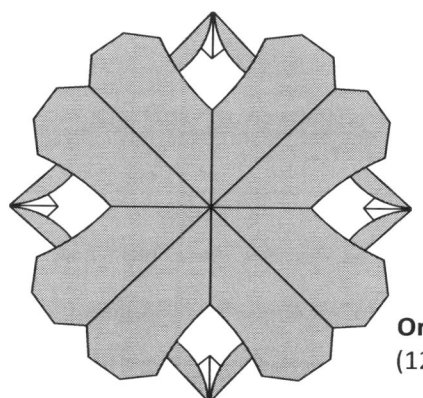

Origami My Heart
(12-unit assembly)

30-unit Assembly

Join 3 more units in a ring following steps *2,3,4* and *5*. Add a sixth unit following steps *6* and *7*. Continue forming groups of 5 (where flowers form) and groups of 3 (where holes form) in an icosahedral symmetry to complete assembly.

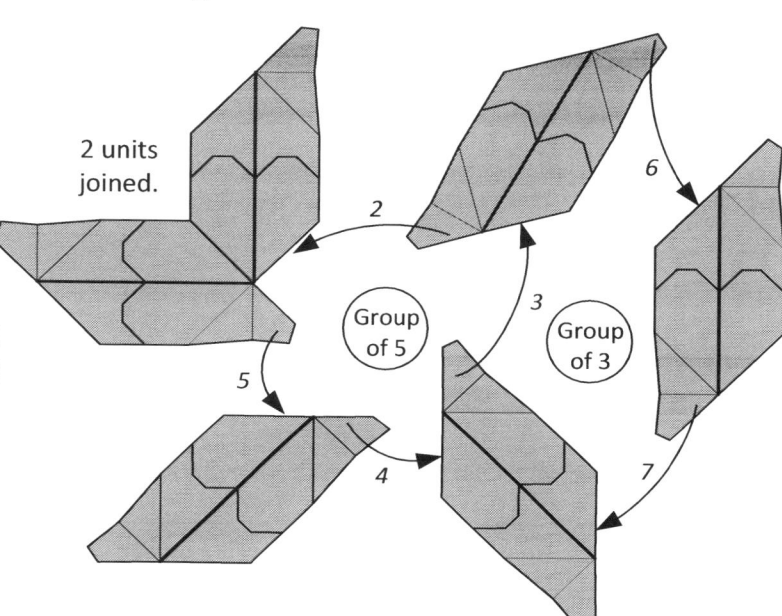

(For video help please go to youtube.com/watch?v=HSquJKFRWnw)

Origami My Heart
(30-unit assembly)

(Photo on cover, bottom left)

Exquisite Modular Origami II

Heart Petals

(Created April 2014)

Obtain the starting paper ratio of 2:3 rectangles as explained on page 7.

Use printer paper, or Tant, or paper of similar weight.

1. Start with 2:3 rectangle and fold quarters.

2. Pinch half and quarter points of the flaps.

3. Mountain fold in half.

4. Fold the 2 corners at about 1/3 points. Unfold all.

5. Re-crease diamonds as valley folds. Make the 2 new mountain folds.

6. Collapse following gender of the folds to arrive at the next step.

7. Lift front flap to expose the small inner flap shown dotted in X-ray vision. Do not make any new crease.

8. Fold inner flap securely.

9. Bring front flap back down.

Exquisite Modular Origami II

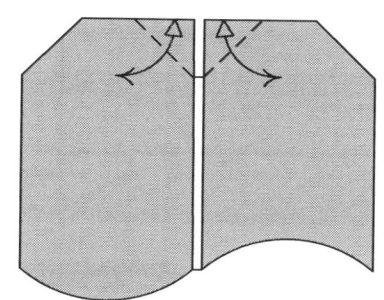

10. Fold the two corners and unfold.

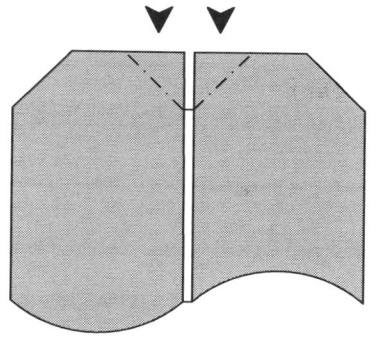

11. Reverse fold along creases just made to complete the lobes of the heart.

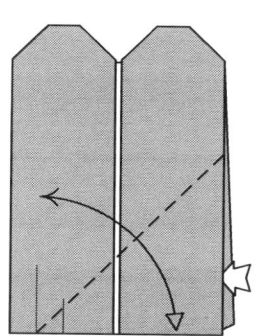

12. Fold front flap and unfold.

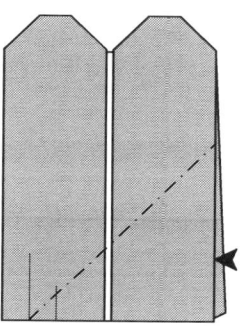

13. Reverse fold along the crease just made.

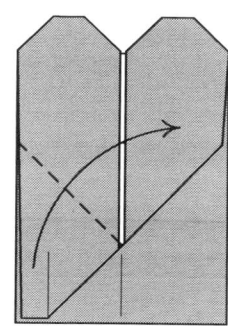

14. Fold front flap.

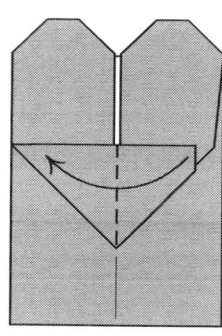

15. Fold front flap.

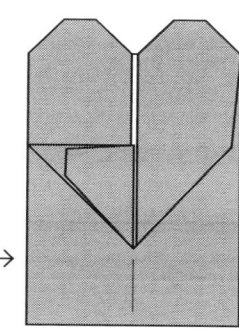

16. Repeat Steps 12-15 at the back.

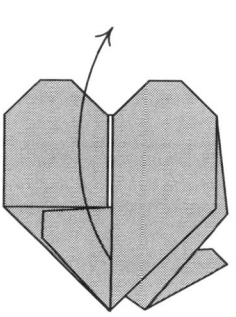

17. Lift the front heart without creasing lobes.

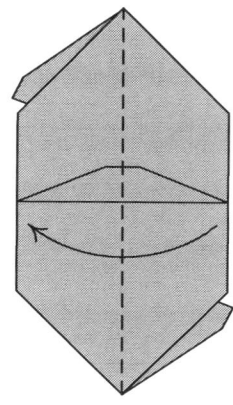

18. Re-crease firmly through all layers. Make sure that the middle flap is oriented with its plain side visible.

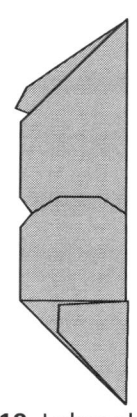

19. Lobes should be perpendicular to unit. Unfold unit slightly.

Finished Unit x12 or x30

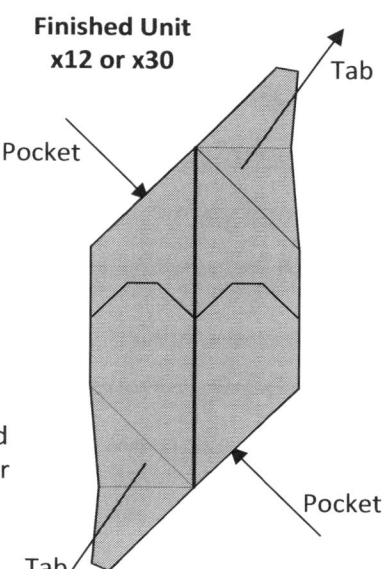

Exquisite Modular Origami II

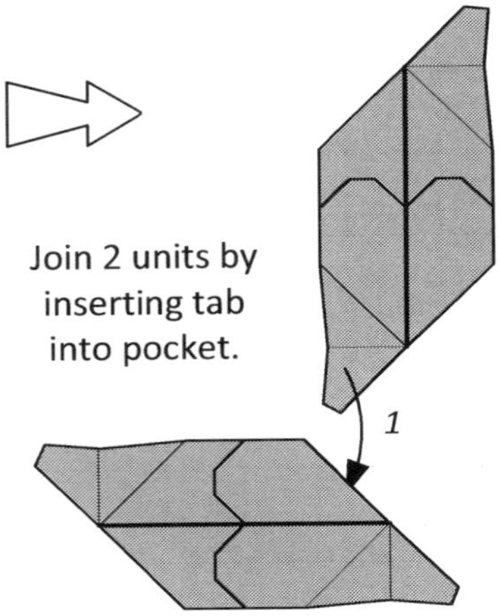

Join 2 units by inserting tab into pocket.

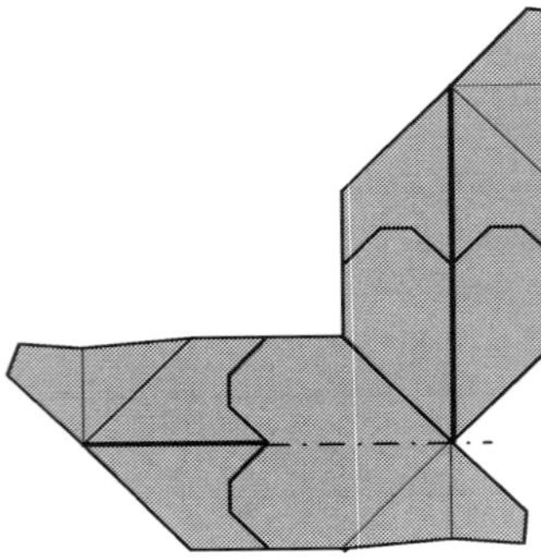

Reinforce the mountain fold through layers of both units to lock securely. You may need to repeat this several times during the assembly process.

12 and 30 unit assemblies of Heart Petals

Assemble 12 or 30 units exactly like the previous model, Origami My Heart. Although the two models look identical, there are enough differences in the steps that may be of interest to folders from the design perspective. Origami my Heart starts with rectangles whereas Heart Petals start with squares. Also, the latter has fewer steps and hence is faster to fold.

Two views of a 12- Unit assembly of Heart Petals

Exquisite Modular Origami II

Ornamental Omega 5

(Created March 2012)

This design is inspired by Michael Naughton's Ornamental Omega Star, being merely its pentagonal version. Michael has kindly granted me permission to diagram and publish this variation, so many thanks to him. The original Omega Star can be jointly attributed to Philip Shen and Ed Sullivan.

We will start by showing Toyoaki Kawai's method of obtaining a pentagon from a square used in this model. If you have any other favorite method, please go ahead and use it.

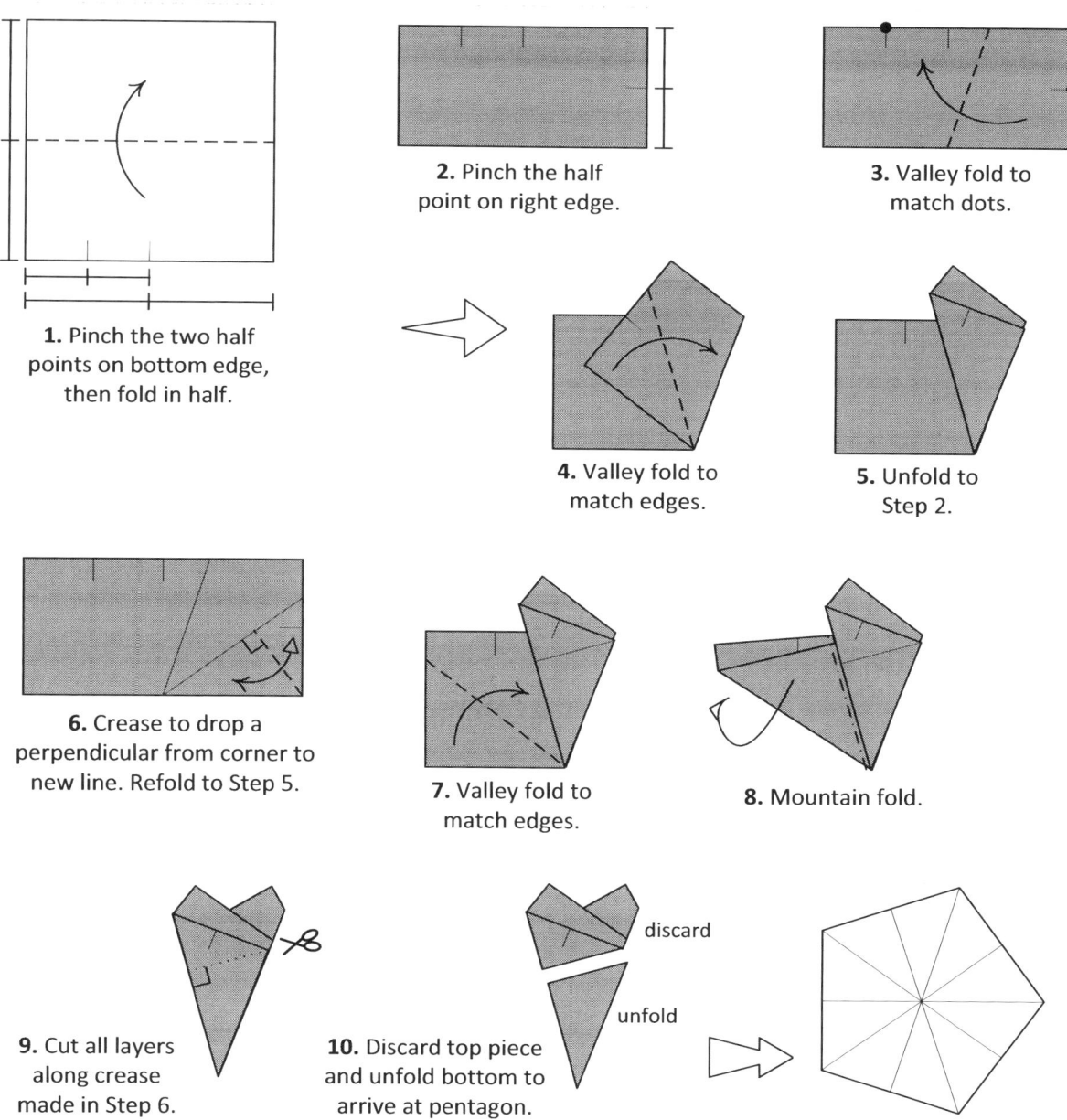

1. Pinch the two half points on bottom edge, then fold in half.
2. Pinch the half point on right edge.
3. Valley fold to match dots.
4. Valley fold to match edges.
5. Unfold to Step 2.
6. Crease to drop a perpendicular from corner to new line. Refold to Step 5.
7. Valley fold to match edges.
8. Mountain fold.
9. Cut all layers along crease made in Step 6.
10. Discard top piece and unfold bottom to arrive at pentagon.

Exquisite Modular Origami II

Making the units: Start with a pentagon made by using the method explained on the previous page.

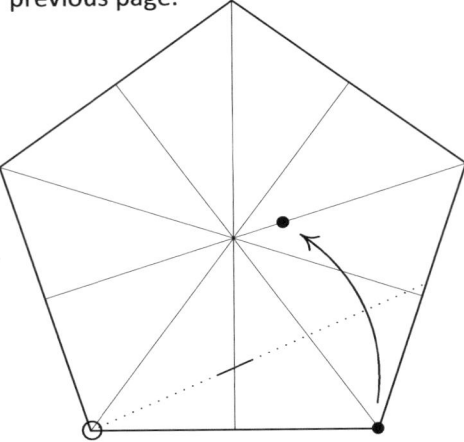

1. Lift bottom edge and rotate with circled point as pivot to match dots. Make a pinch on the vertical axis.

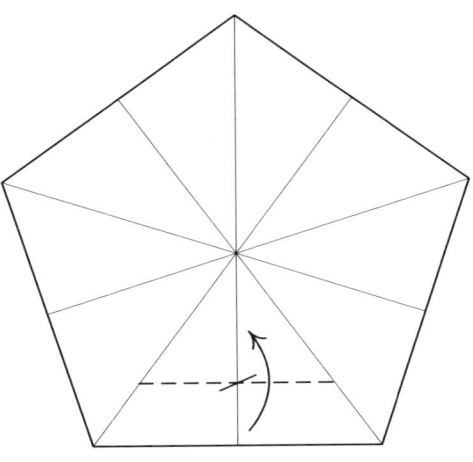

2. Fold a horizontal line through the pinch mark, creasing only the section shown.

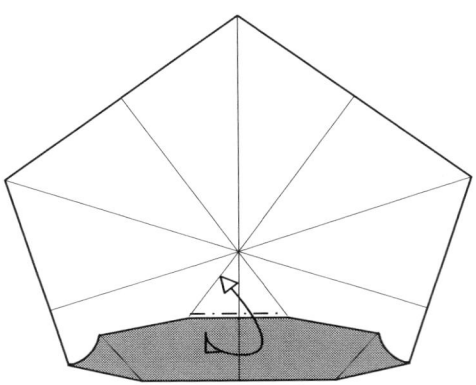

3. Mountain fold and unfold along edge only in the section shown.

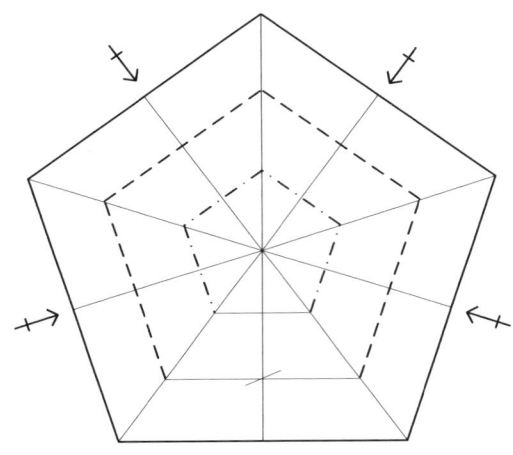

4. Using the creases from Steps 2 and 3 as references, complete creasing an outer and an inner pentagon, in valley and mountain folds respectively.

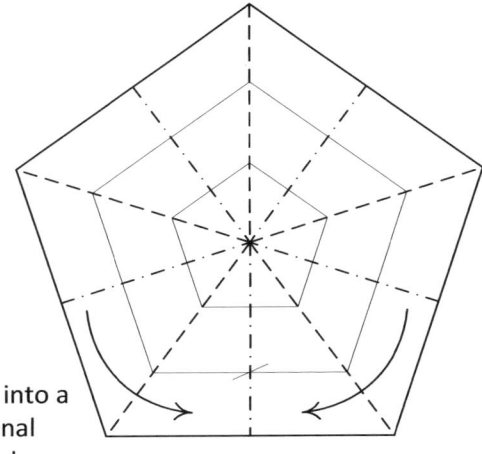

5. Collapse into a pentagonal waterbomb base.

6. Sink using preexisting creases of outer pentagon.

Exquisite Modular Origami II

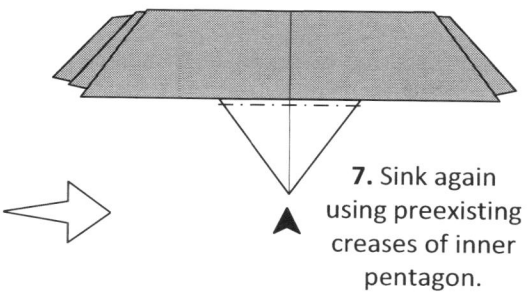

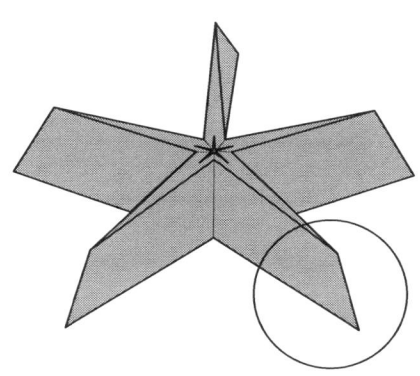

7. Sink again using preexisting creases of inner pentagon.

8. The unit is now 3D and has 5 arms.

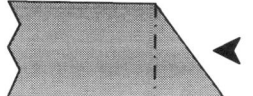

9. This picture shows one arm. Reverse fold tip. Repeat on all four other arms.

Finished Unit x12

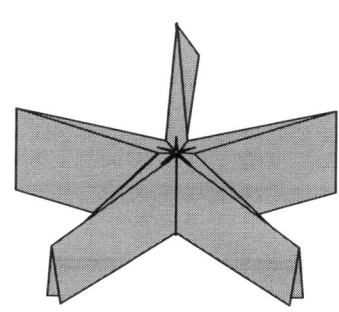

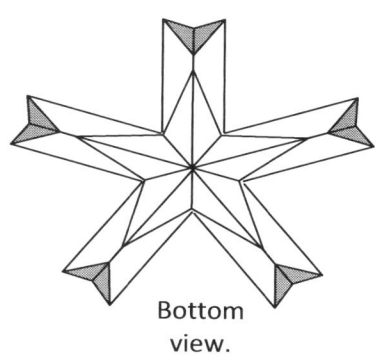

Bottom view.

Assembly

1. Take one arm of one unit, *A*, and unfold the reverse fold from Step 8.

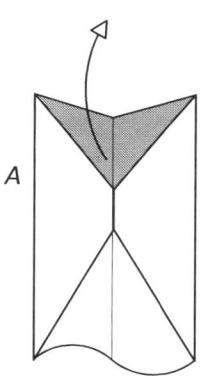

2. Take one arm of another unit, *B*, and insert into *A* on one side of the inner star.

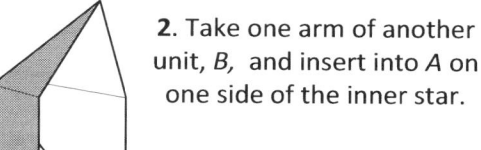

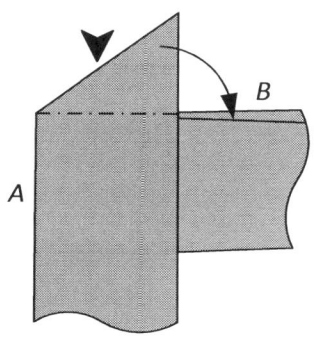

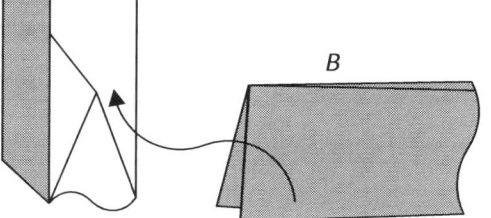

3. Redo the reverse fold so the tip of *A* goes into the slot of *B*. Note that this will join two arms but not yet lock them.

Exquisite Modular Origami II

4. Join a third unit as shown using the same method as Steps 1-3.

5. This figure shows only the six arms that we just joined. Valley fold as shown to lock the arms together.

6. Six locked arms. Notice how the inner stars of the units get exposed.

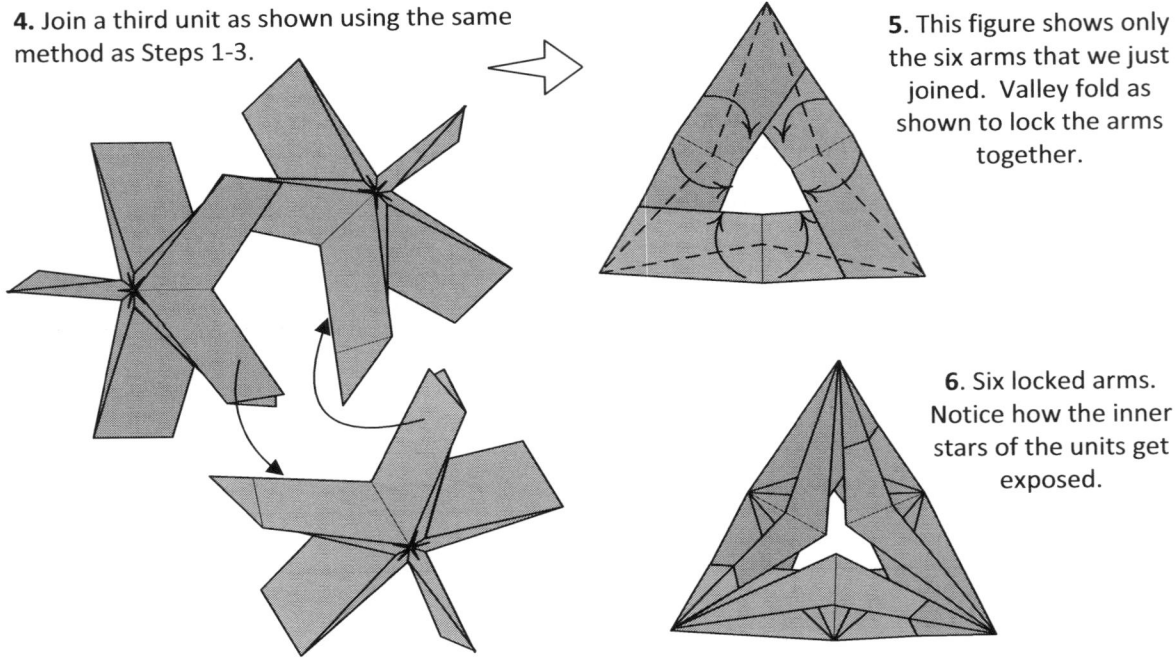

7. To assemble all 12 units, construct such that each unit lies along the pentagonal face of an icosidodecahedron, and at each triangular face, 6 arms from 3 units lock as above. As you have noticed, each arm has the potential of being either a tab or a pocket. Since the total number of tabs and pockets per unit is odd (5), the tab-pocket distribution for every unit will not be even across the model. But it is recommended that you use the units in such a way that each one has either 3 tabs and 2 pockets or has 2 tabs and 3 pockets, to attain some homogeneity in the tab-pocket distribution.

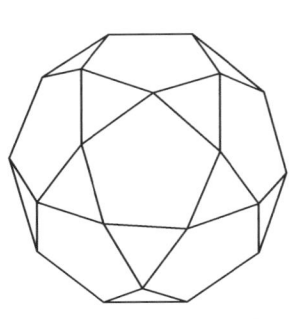

The underlying symmetry will be that of an icosidodecahedron.

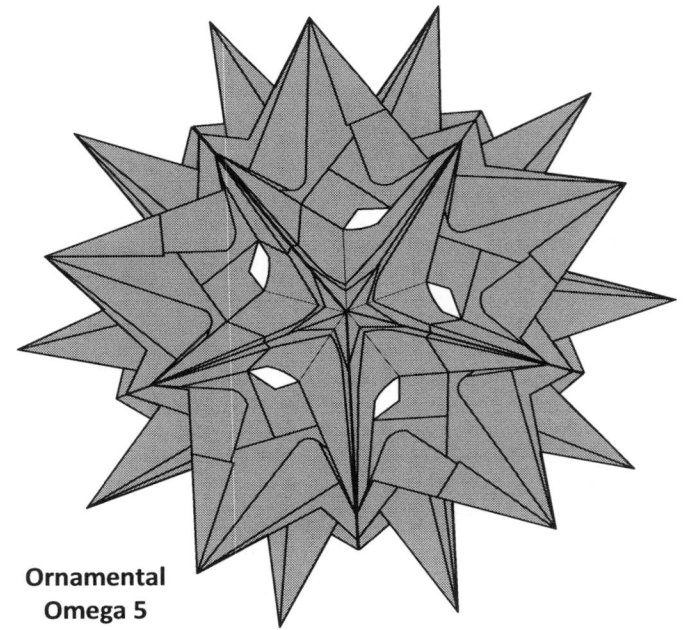

Ornamental Omega 5

(Photo on cover, top left)

Exquisite Modular Origami II

Compound of Five Tetrahedra

(Created September 2014)

This interesting compound is also called the 47th Stellation of the Icosahedron. Inspired by Tom Hull's 1997 Challenge (http://mars.wne.edu/~thull/fit.html), I revisited the solid version for a second time. My previous attempt about a decade ago was not sturdy so I improved upon it. There are a handful of solutions by others as well, Kamiya Satoshi, Barlaham Benitez Vargas and Nicolás Gajardo Henríquez, to name a few. But these are from rectangles instead of squares. Also, my units are relatively easier to fold with fewer steps.

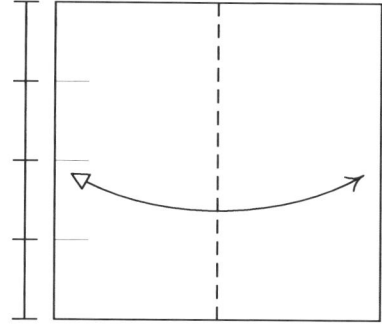

1. Book fold and unfold. Pinch half and quarter points on the left.

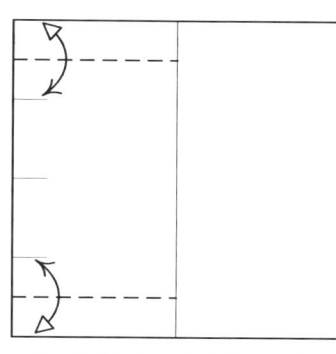

2. Fold the eighths only halfway and unfold.

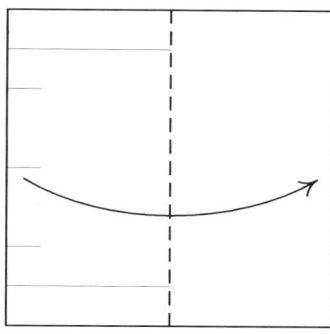

3. Re-fold into half.

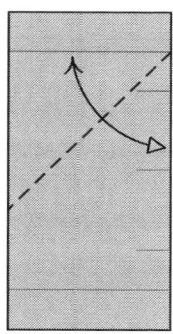

4. Fold edge to line, then unfold all.

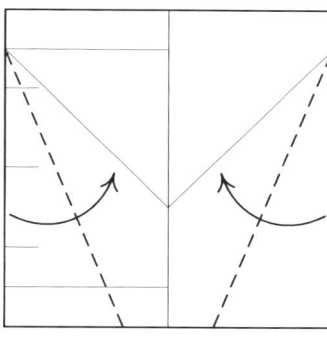

5. Fold right edge and then left.

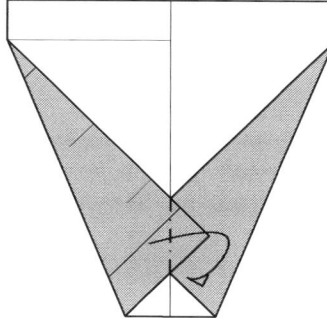

6. Fold left flap back along the centerfold.

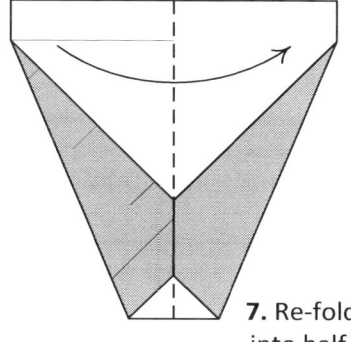

7. Re-fold into half.

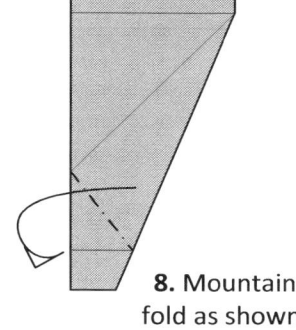

8. Mountain fold as shown.

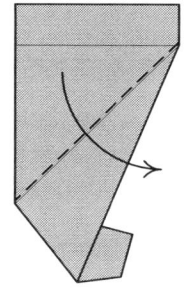

9. Fold at the existing crease.

Exquisite Modular Origami II

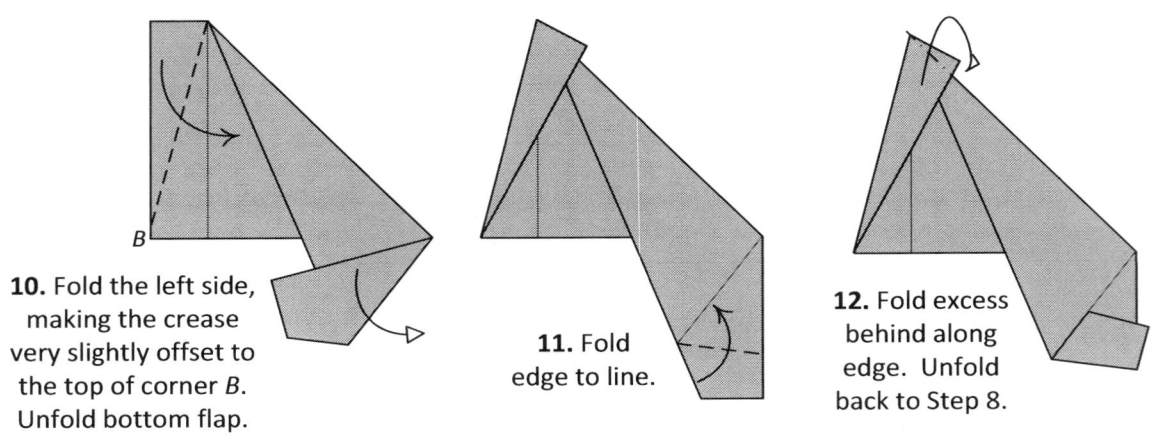

10. Fold the left side, making the crease very slightly offset to the top of corner *B*. Unfold bottom flap.

11. Fold edge to line.

12. Fold excess behind along edge. Unfold back to Step 8.

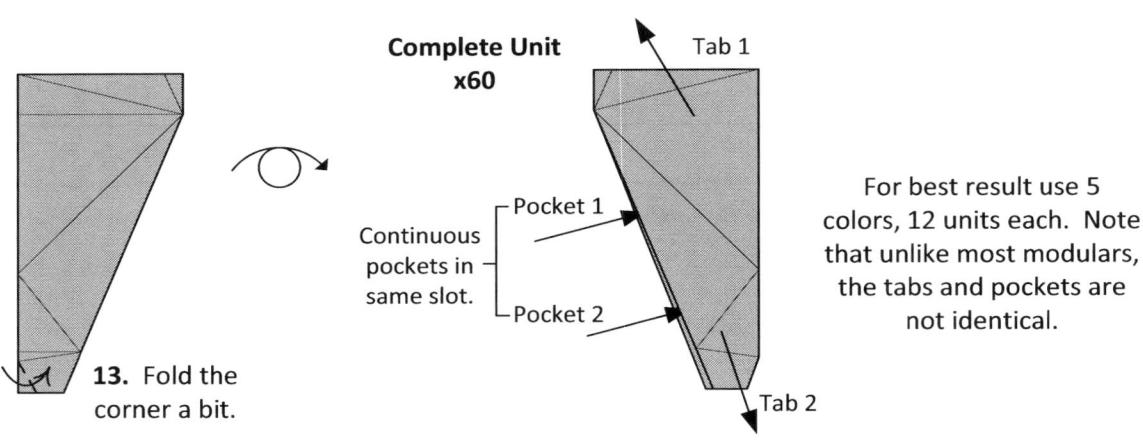

Complete Unit x60

Continuous pockets in same slot.

Pocket 1
Pocket 2
Tab 1
Tab 2

13. Fold the corner a bit.

For best result use 5 colors, 12 units each. Note that unlike most modulars, the tabs and pockets are not identical.

Assembly

Before we assemble anything we will discuss two kinds of joints illustrated next.

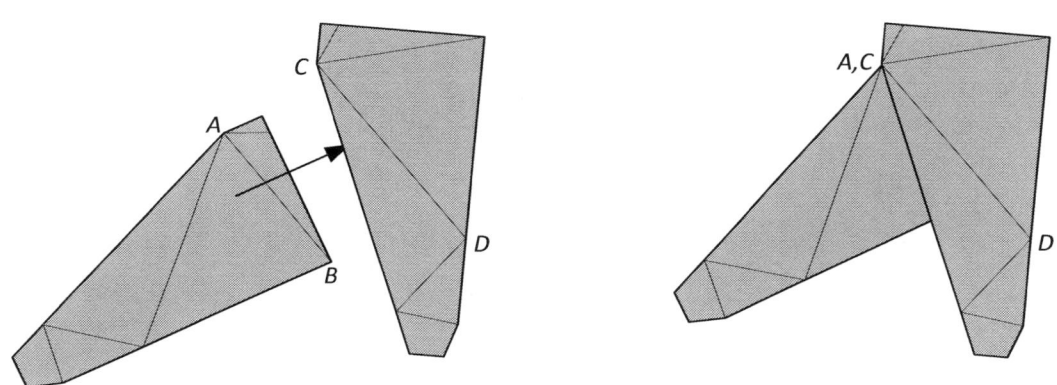

Joint 1: Take two units of like colors and insert Tab 1 into Pocket 1 such that *AB* aligns with *CD* and *A* coincides with *C*.

Exquisite Modular Origami II

Joint 2: Take two units of different colors and insert Tab 2 into Pocket 2 such that *PQ* aligns with *RS* and *Q* coincides with *S*.

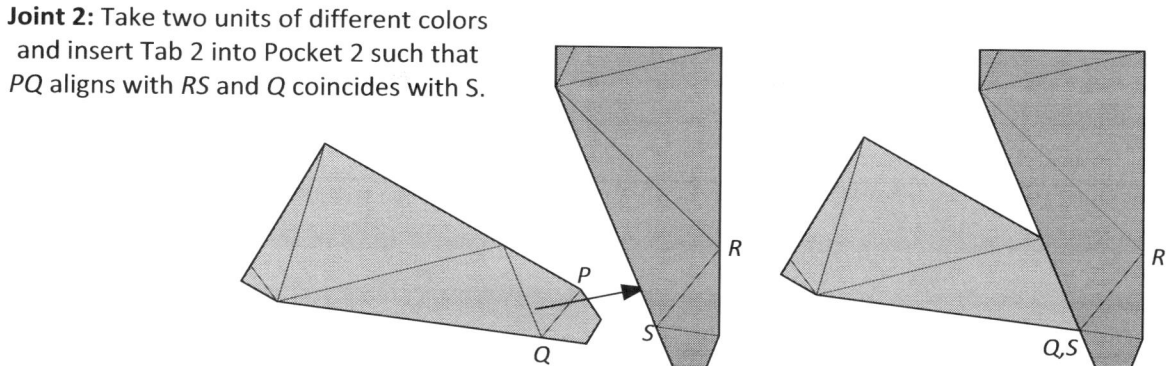

The recommendation would be to first construct all 20 vertices/pyramids of the tetrahedra, four of each of the five colors and then put them together to finish the compound.

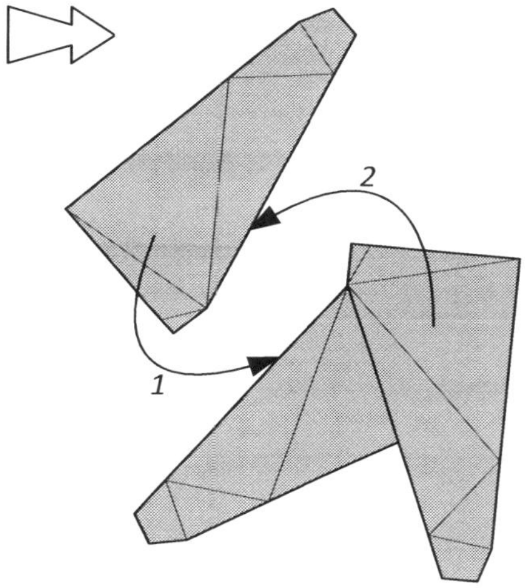

To construct a pyramid, join 3 units using joint type 1.

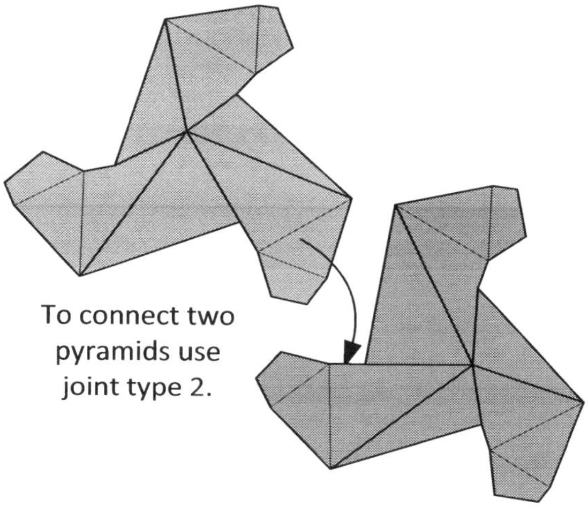

To connect two pyramids use joint type 2.

Construct 20 pyramids using joint type 1. Next, join the 20 pyramids using joint type 2. Carefully place the colors at the vertices of the respective tetrahedron they are a part of, to arrive at the finished compound.

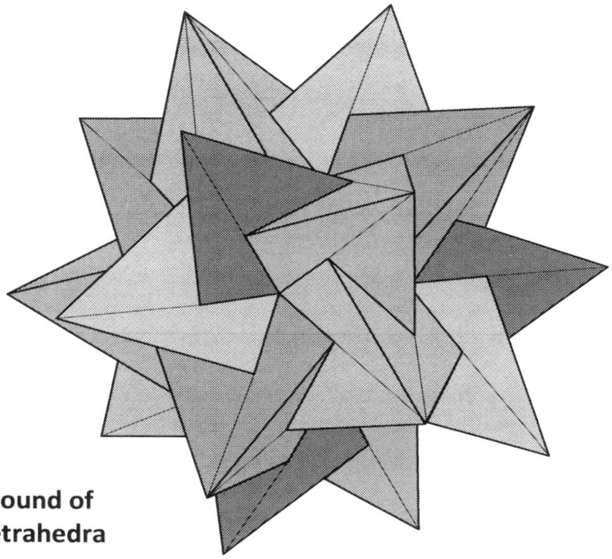

Compound of Five Tetrahedra

(Photo on cover, top right)

Ornamental Cube

(Created June 2011)

This design borrows techniques from Shuzo Fujimoto's famous Hydrangea. Fujimoto san has graciously granted me permission to publish the diagrams for this cube. Since Hydrangea diagrams as well as video instructions are available on the Internet, I am not going to redraw in detail. For your reference, here are sources for folding the Hydrangea*:
- Video by Sara Adams: https://www.youtube.com/watch?v=zu5F0Hmd3ZA
- Diagrams by John Smith:
  http://www.nickrobinson.info/clients/smithy/hydrangea_john_smith.pdf

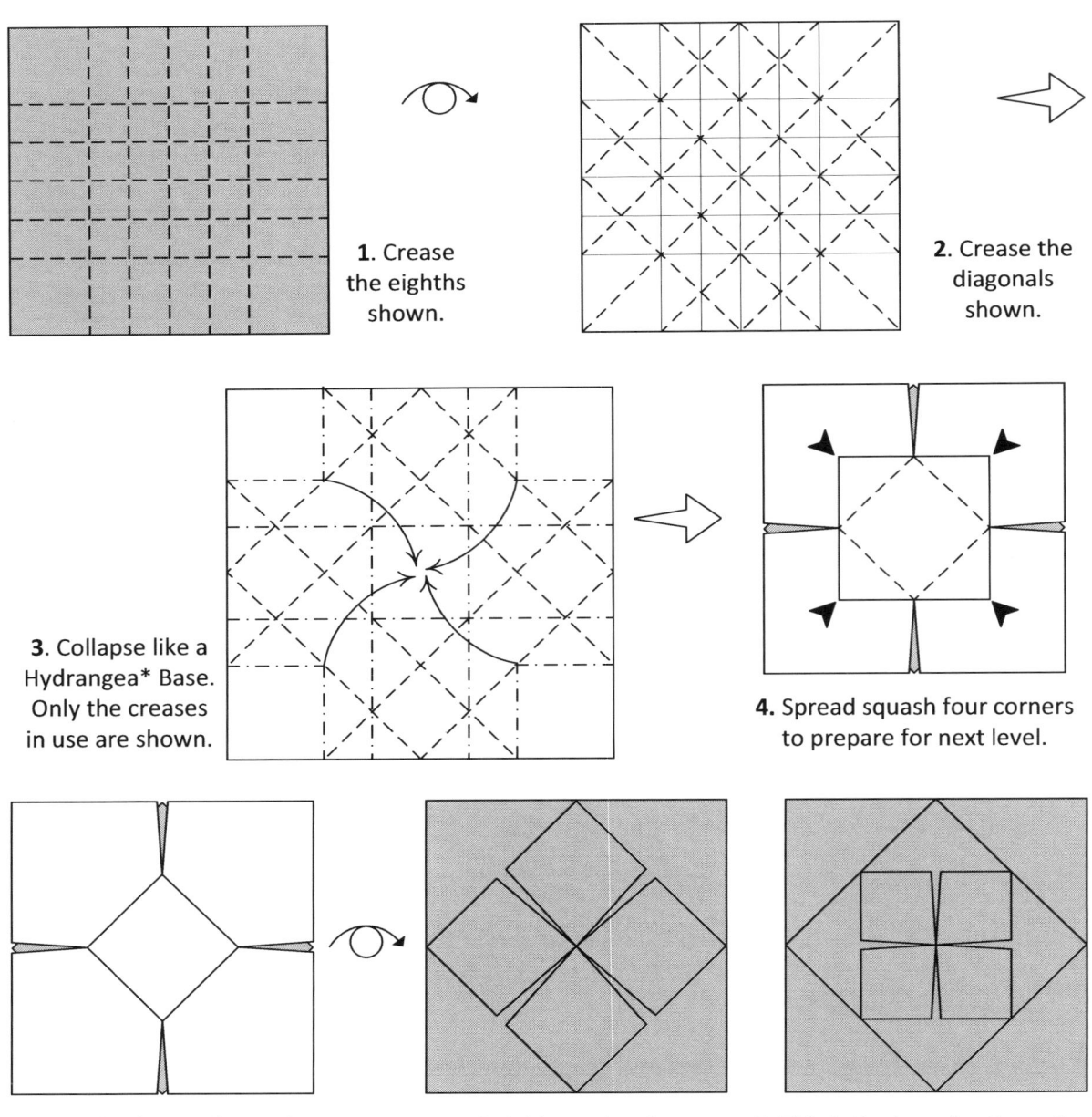

1. Crease the eighths shown.

2. Crease the diagonals shown.

3. Collapse like a Hydrangea* Base. Only the creases in use are shown.

4. Spread squash four corners to prepare for next level.

5. Result of spread squashes.

6. Add next level.

7. This is the base for the unit.

Exquisite Modular Origami II

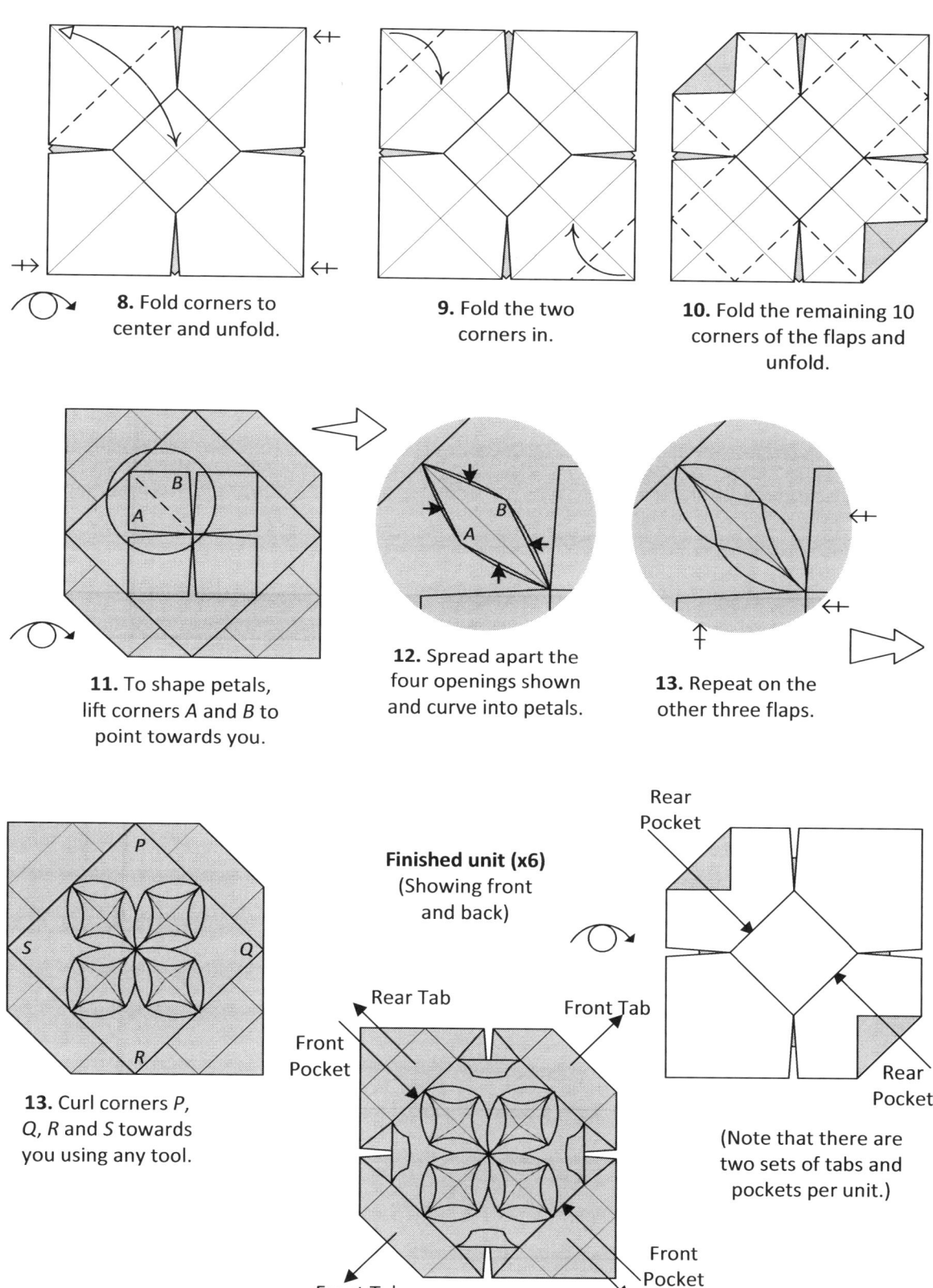

Assembly

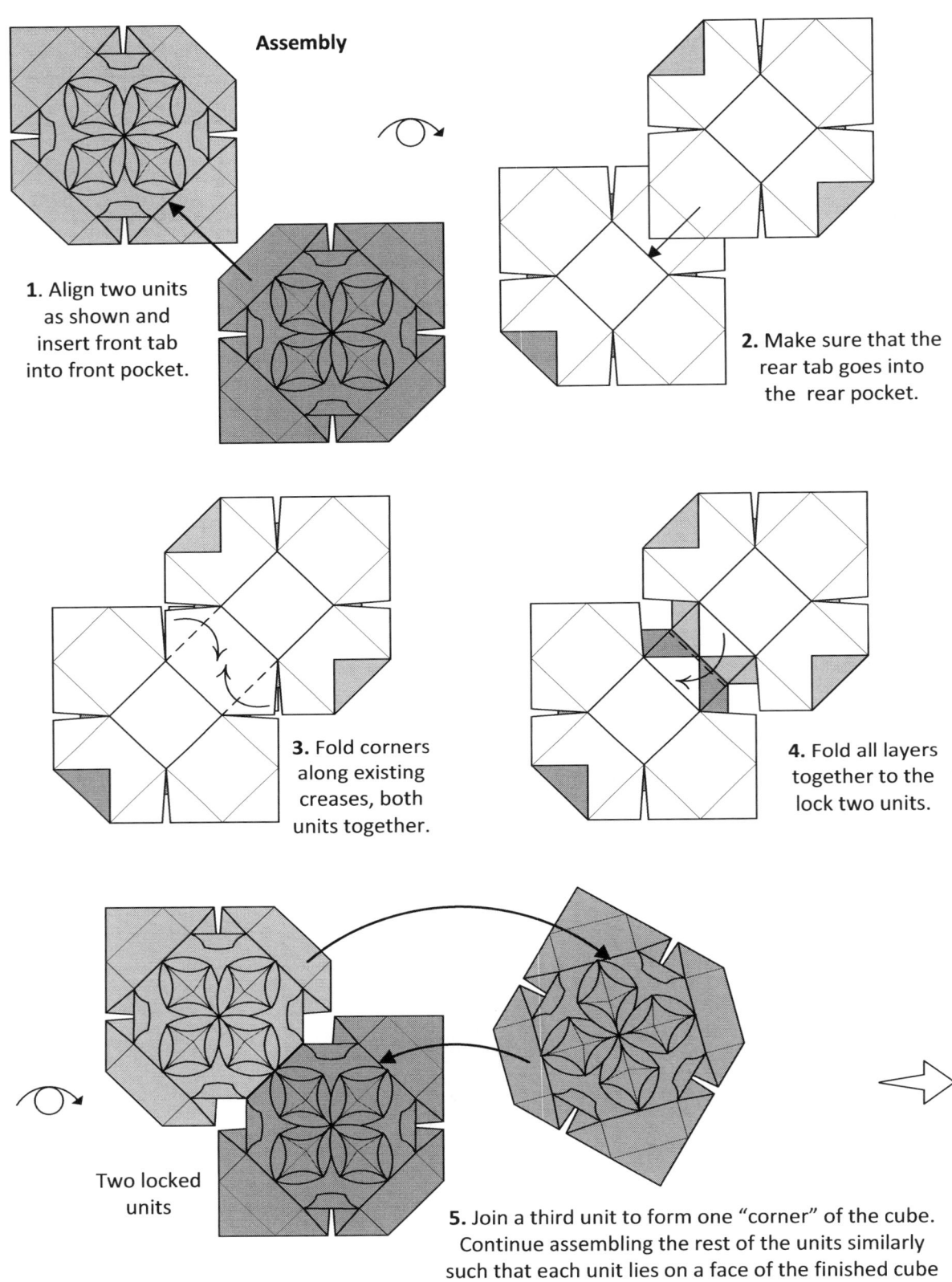

1. Align two units as shown and insert front tab into front pocket.

2. Make sure that the rear tab goes into the rear pocket.

3. Fold corners along existing creases, both units together.

4. Fold all layers together to the lock two units.

Two locked units

5. Join a third unit to form one "corner" of the cube. Continue assembling the rest of the units similarly such that each unit lies on a face of the finished cube and each locked joint lies on an edge of the cube.

(Photo on cover, top middle)

Exquisite Modular Origami II

Ornamental Cube

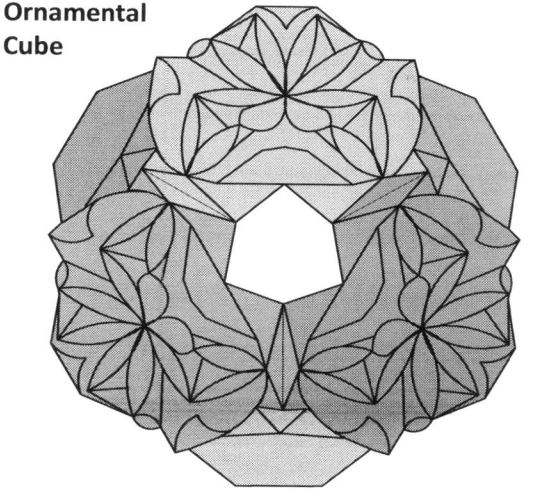

(Photo on cover, top row, middle)

Variations: The finishes of the outer and inner layers may be varied for different looks.

Instead of curling the corners in Step 13, shape them as shown for a different outer layer.

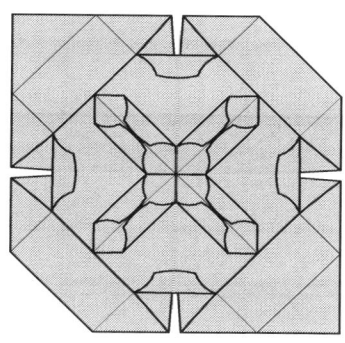

These easy variations may be applied to the inner layer and combined with any of the two outer layer finishes discussed earlier for various looks.

Hydrangea Cube

Make 6 Hydrangeas of any number of levels and join them exactly as the Ornamental Cube to get a Hydrangea Cube. If you make an odd number of levels, the rear pockets will be just like the Ornamental Cube. However, if you make an even number of levels, the rear pockets will be at the corners of the innermost square in the rear.

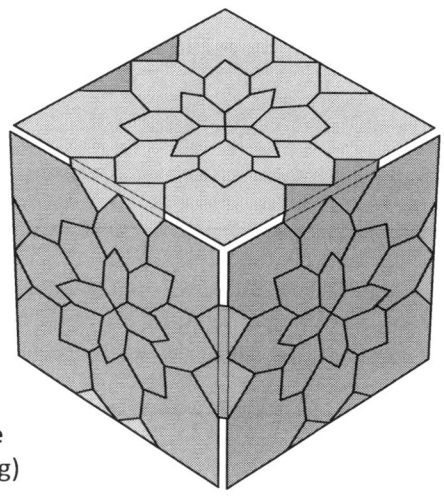

5-Level Hydrangea Cube
(First level used for locking)

(Photo on page vi)

Exquisite Modular Origami II

Dogwood Cube and Flower

(Created April 2015)

For best results, use Corona Harmony paper, 6" or larger. You can find additional collapse help for Hydrangea Base or Crossed Box Pleat on the Internet, see links listed on page 66.

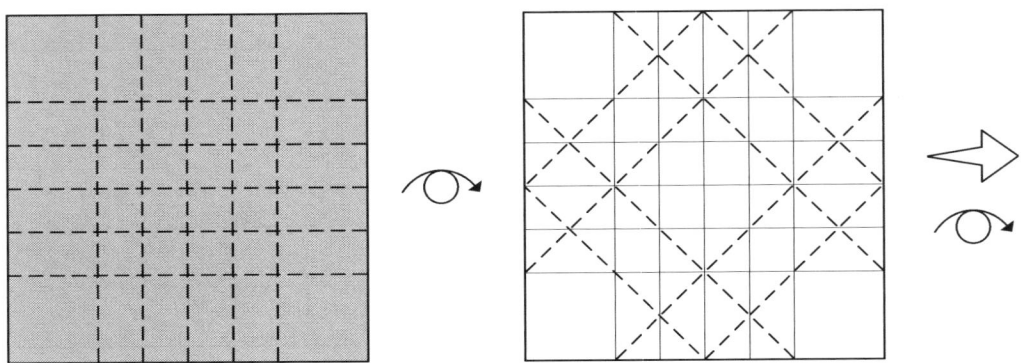

1. Crease the eighths shown.

2. Crease the diagonals shown.

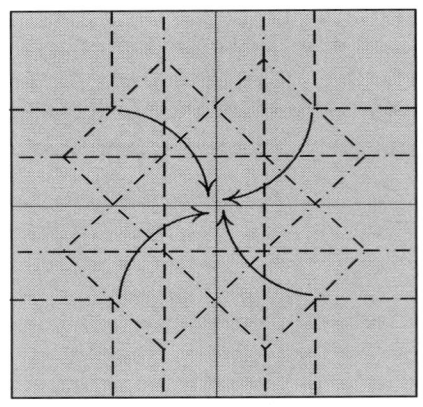

3. Collapse into a crossed box pleat following gender of the folds.

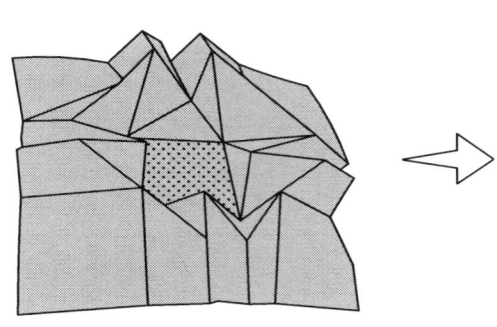

4. Collapse in progress

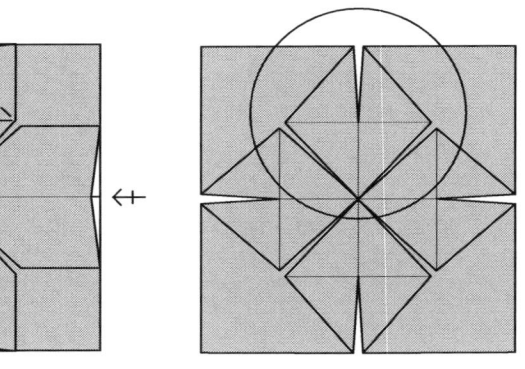

5. Squash the flap and repeat on the other 3.

6. The result.

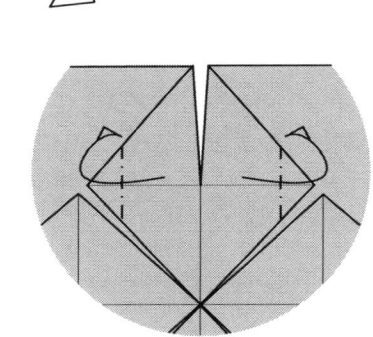

7. Tuck corners firmly.

Exquisite Modular Origami II

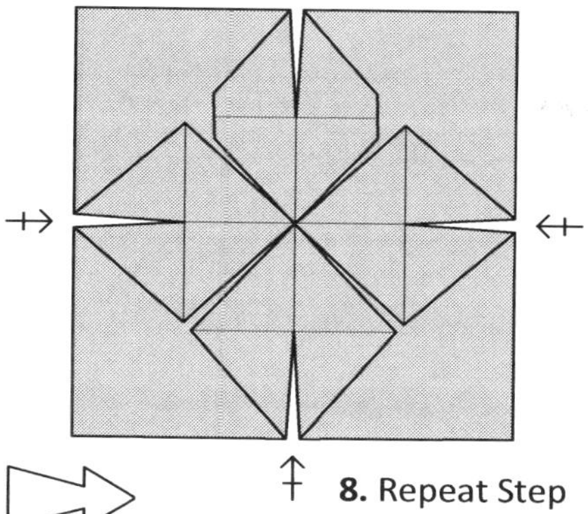

8. Repeat Step 7 all around.

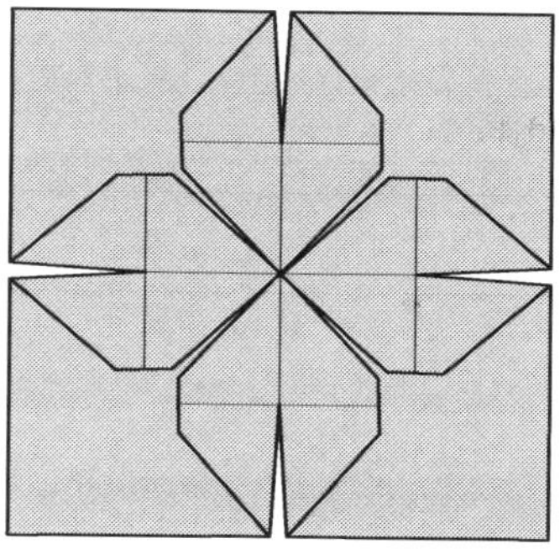

9. Turn over

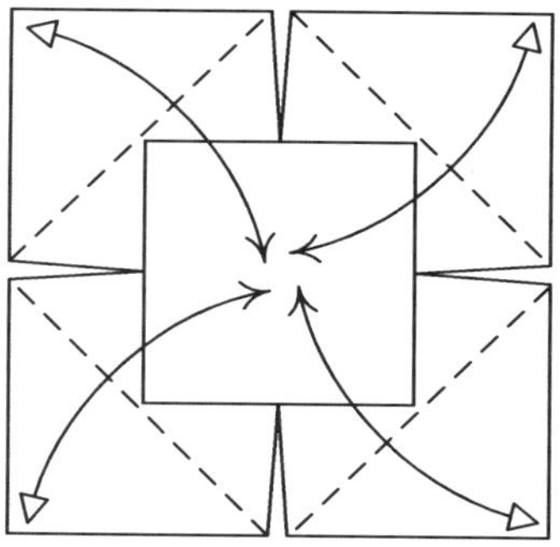

10. Fold corners to center and unfold.

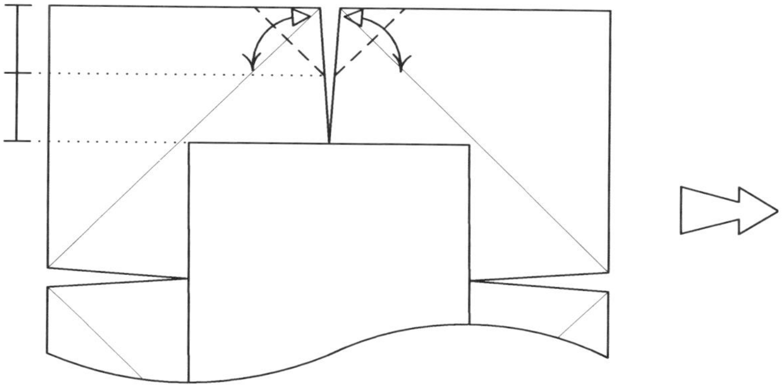

11. Fold the 2 corners shown. The creases begin at about the halfway points of the slit lengths. Unfold. Repeat on other 3 sides.

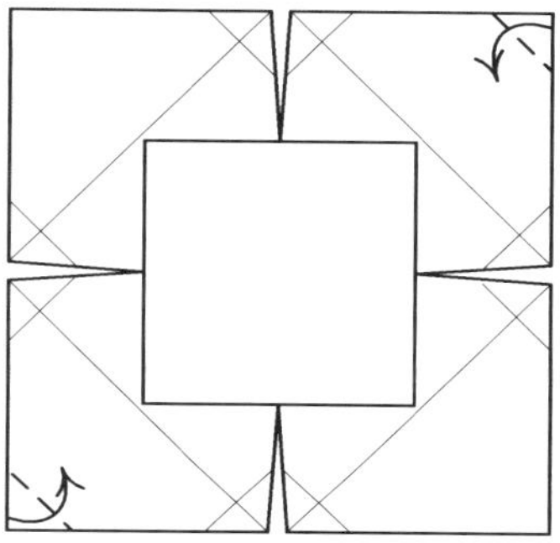

12. Fold the 2 corners a little bit to distinguish Rear Tabs from Front Tabs.

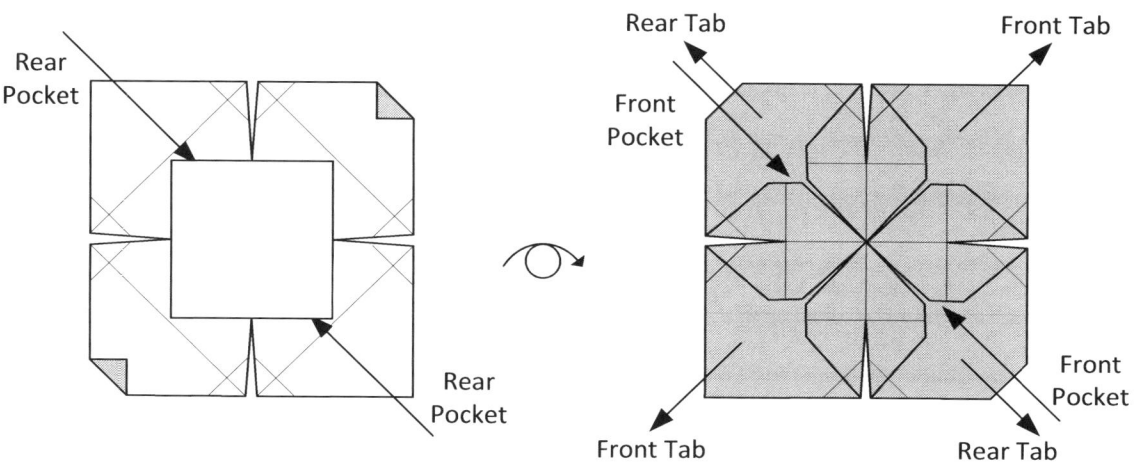

Finished unit (x6)
Showing back and front. (Note that there are two sets of tabs and pockets per unit.)

Exquisite Modular Origami II

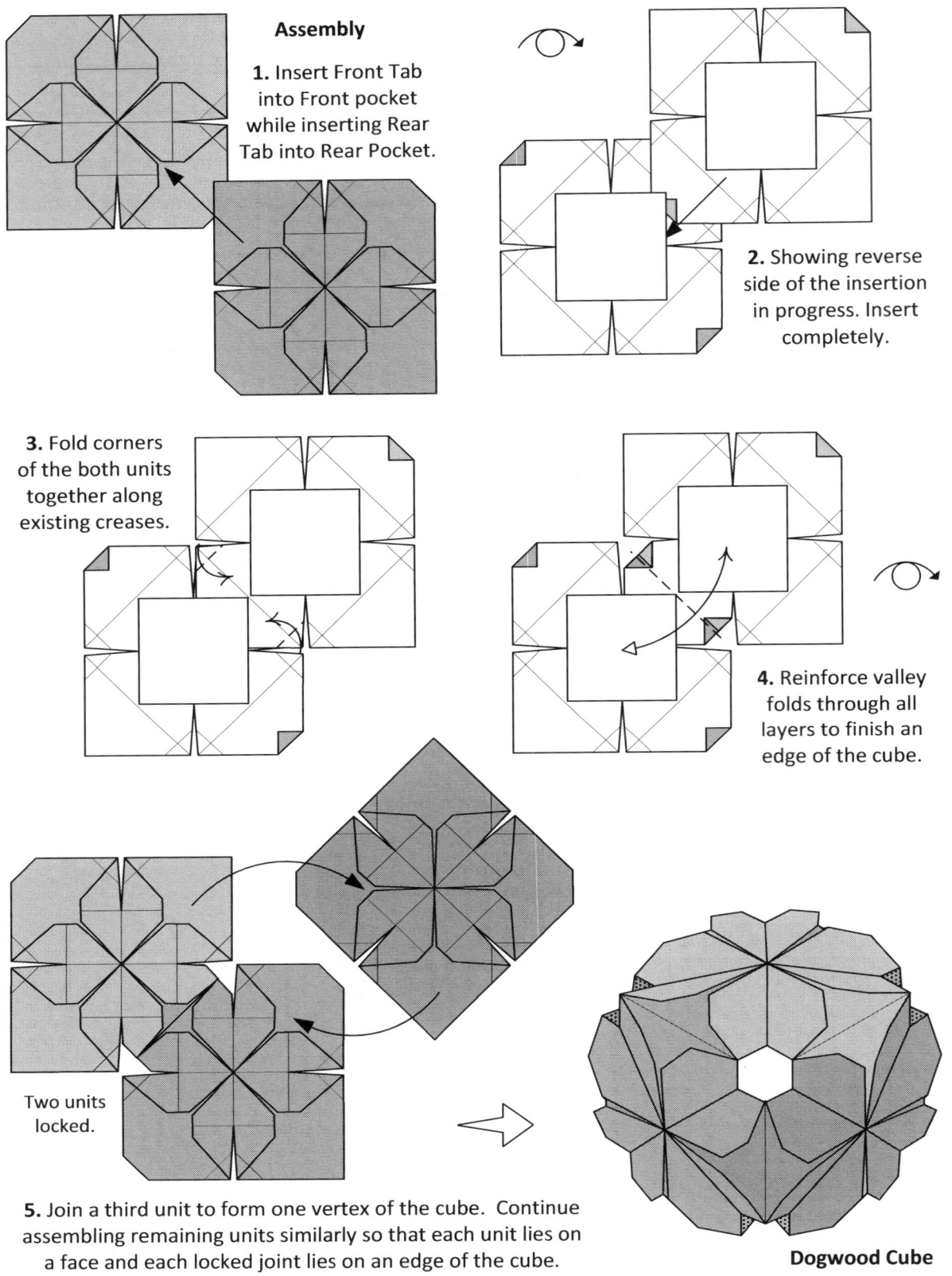

Assembly

1. Insert Front Tab into Front pocket while inserting Rear Tab into Rear Pocket.

2. Showing reverse side of the insertion in progress. Insert completely.

3. Fold corners of the both units together along existing creases.

4. Reinforce valley folds through all layers to finish an edge of the cube.

Two units locked.

5. Join a third unit to form one vertex of the cube. Continue assembling remaining units similarly so that each unit lies on a face and each locked joint lies on an edge of the cube.

Dogwood Cube

(Photo on back cover, third row, right)

Exquisite Modular Origami II

Dogwood Flower and Leaves

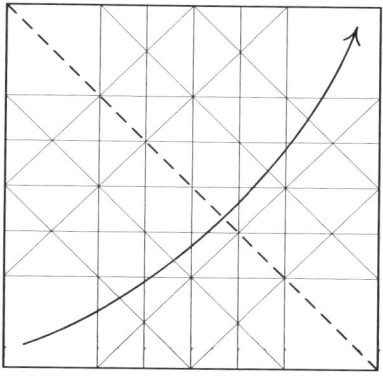

3'. Do Steps 1 and 2 of the Dogwood Cube unit. Fold the diagonal.

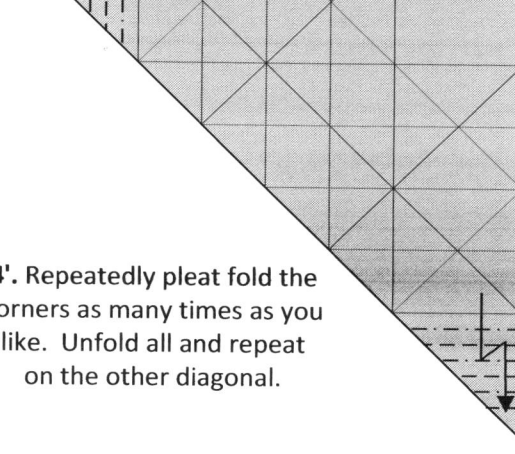

4'. Repeatedly pleat fold the corners as many times as you like. Unfold all and repeat on the other diagonal.

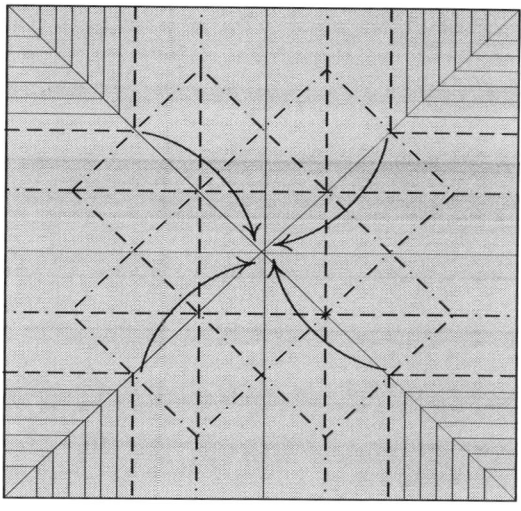

5'. Do Steps 3-11 of Dogwood Cube unit. Do not unfold the folds of Step 11 of the unit.

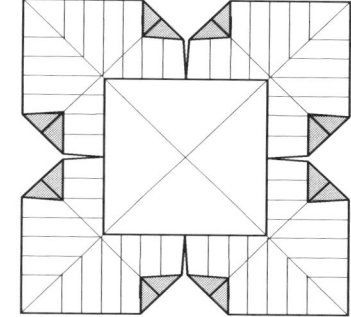

6'. Reinforce the folds of the leaf veins without creasing flower on the reverse.

Dogwood Flower and Leaves

(Yellow and green Corona Harmony paper is recommended)

Exquisite Modular Origami II

Big Dot Cube
(Created April 2015)

To get distinctly colored dots use Corona Harmony paper, 6" or larger.

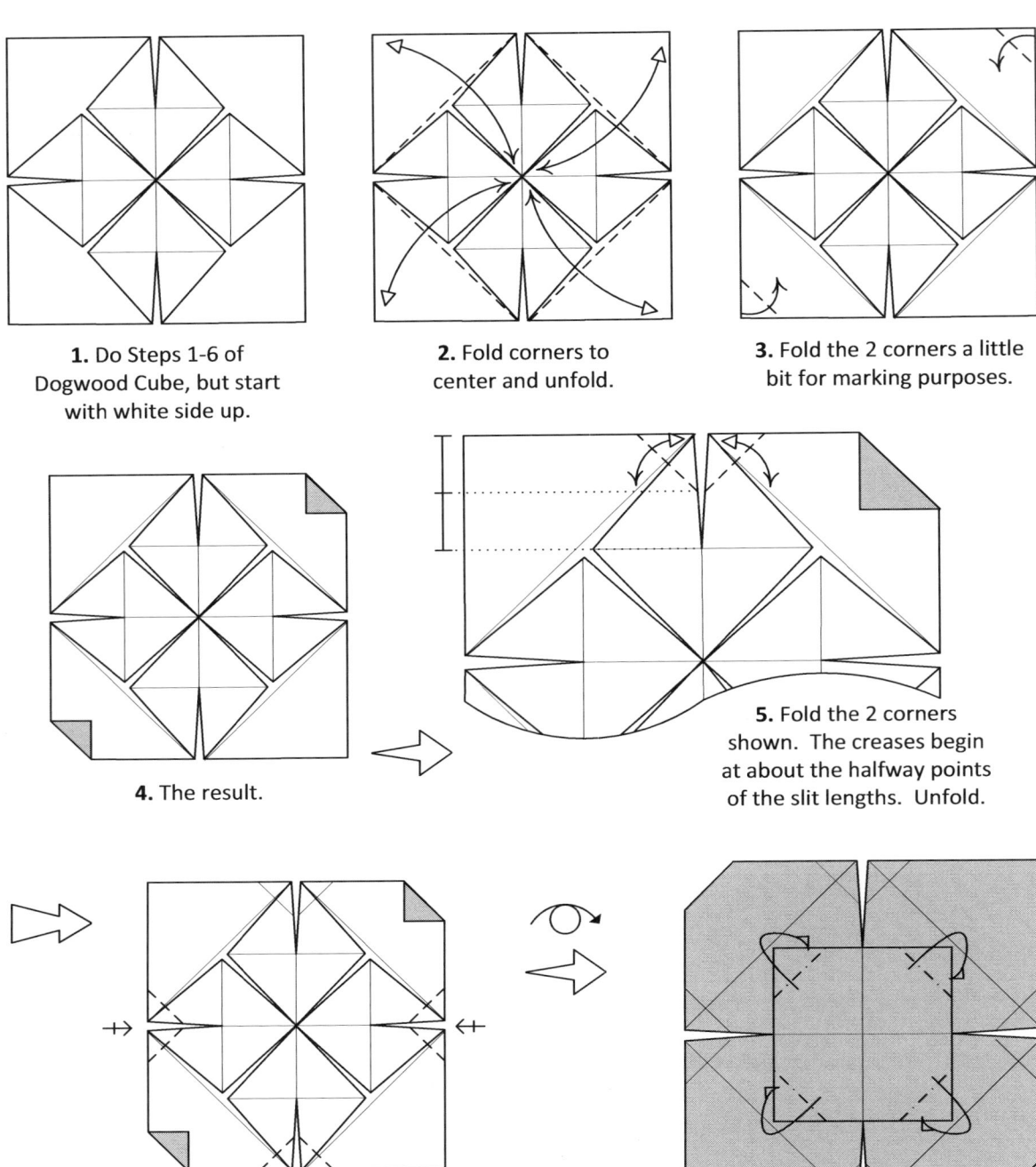

1. Do Steps 1-6 of Dogwood Cube, but start with white side up.

2. Fold corners to center and unfold.

3. Fold the 2 corners a little bit for marking purposes.

4. The result.

5. Fold the 2 corners shown. The creases begin at about the halfway points of the slit lengths. Unfold.

6. Repeat Step 5 on other 3 sides.

7. Fold corners to "round" the square.

Exquisite Modular Origami II

Finished unit (x6) - Showing front and back of the unit.

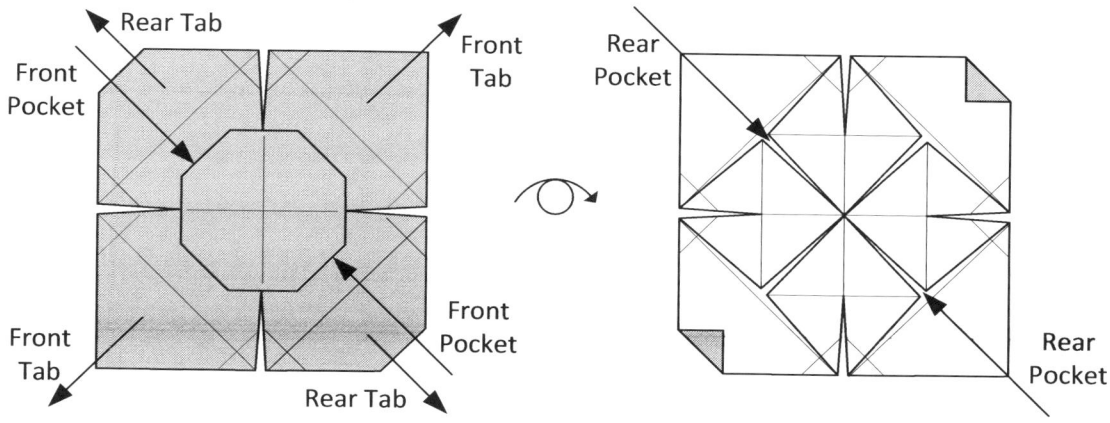

Assembly

1. Insert Front Tab into Front pocket while inserting Rear Tab into Rear Pocket.

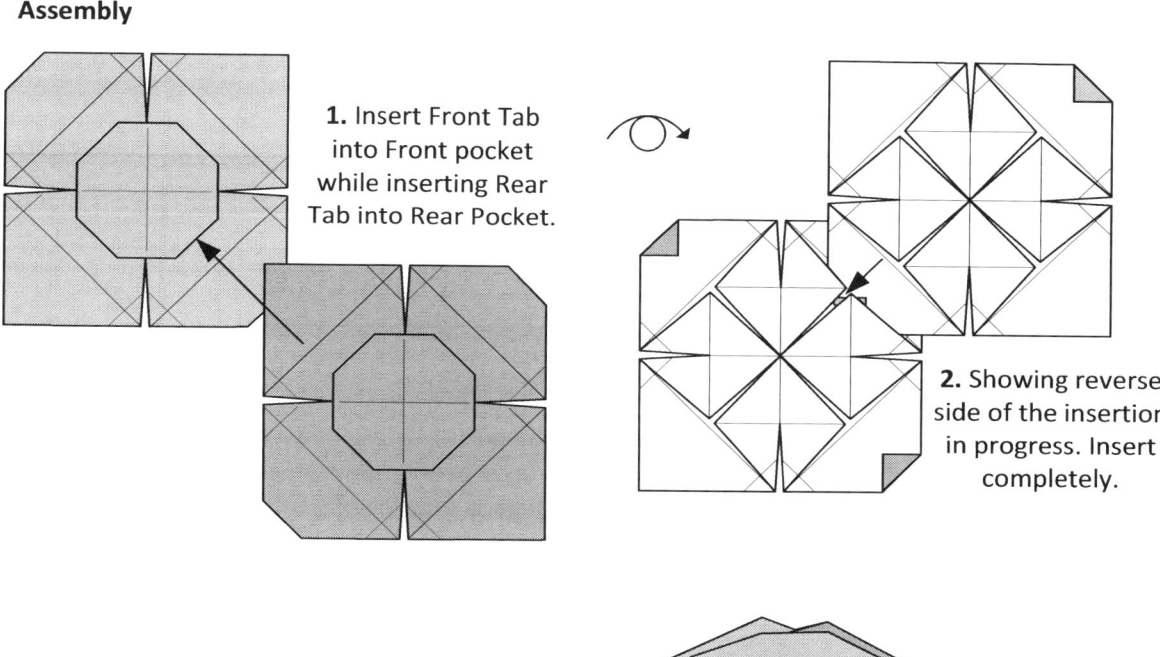

2. Showing reverse side of the insertion in progress. Insert completely.

3. Continue joining and locking exactly like the previous model, the Dogwood Cube, to arrive at your finished model.

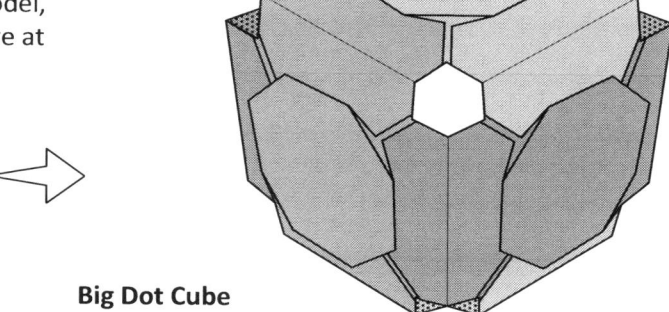

Big Dot Cube

(Photo on back cover, third row, second from right)

Exquisite Modular Origami II

Frangipani

(Designed and diagrammed by Natalia Romanenko, Moldova, March 2013)

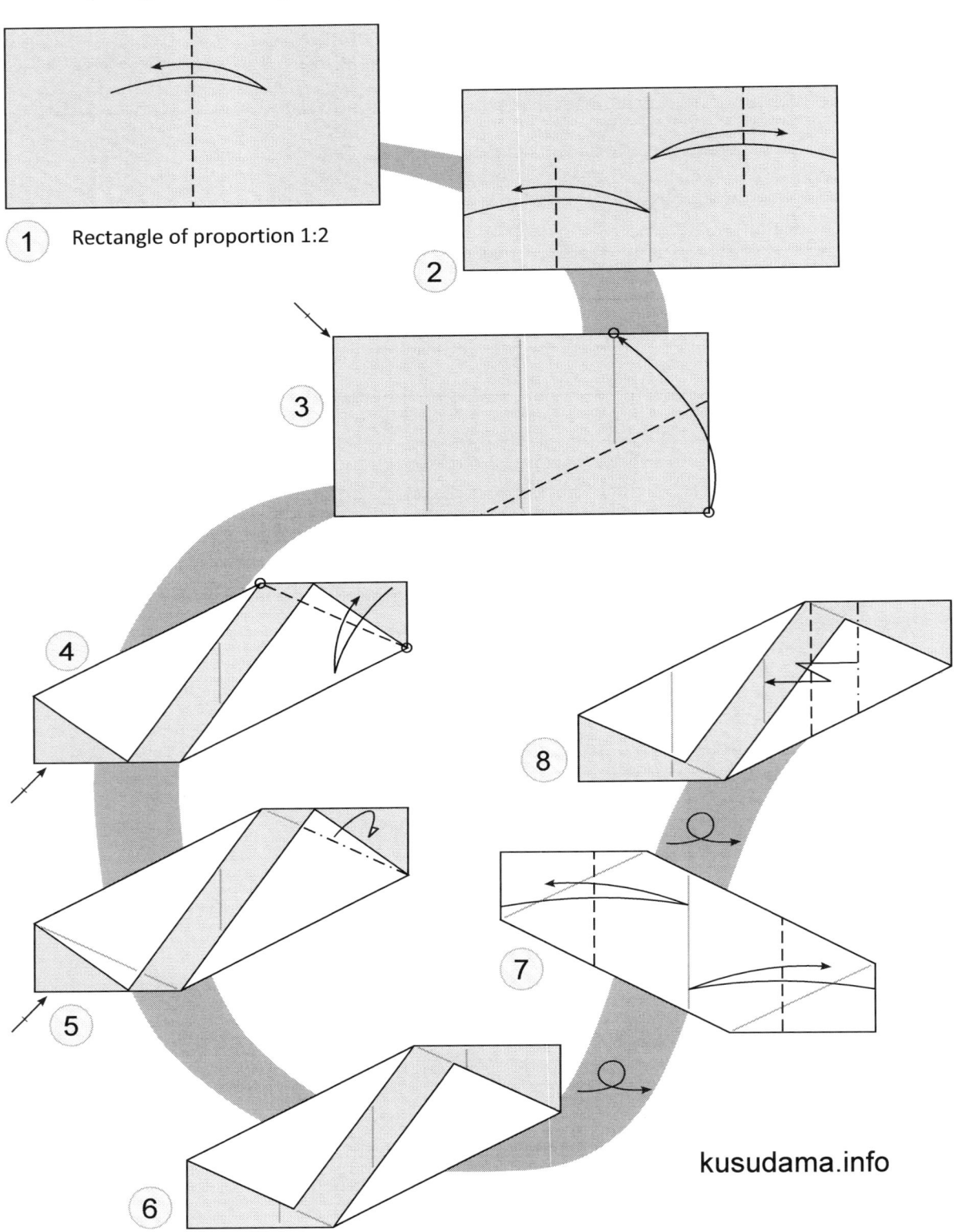

Rectangle of proportion 1:2

Exquisite Modular Origami II

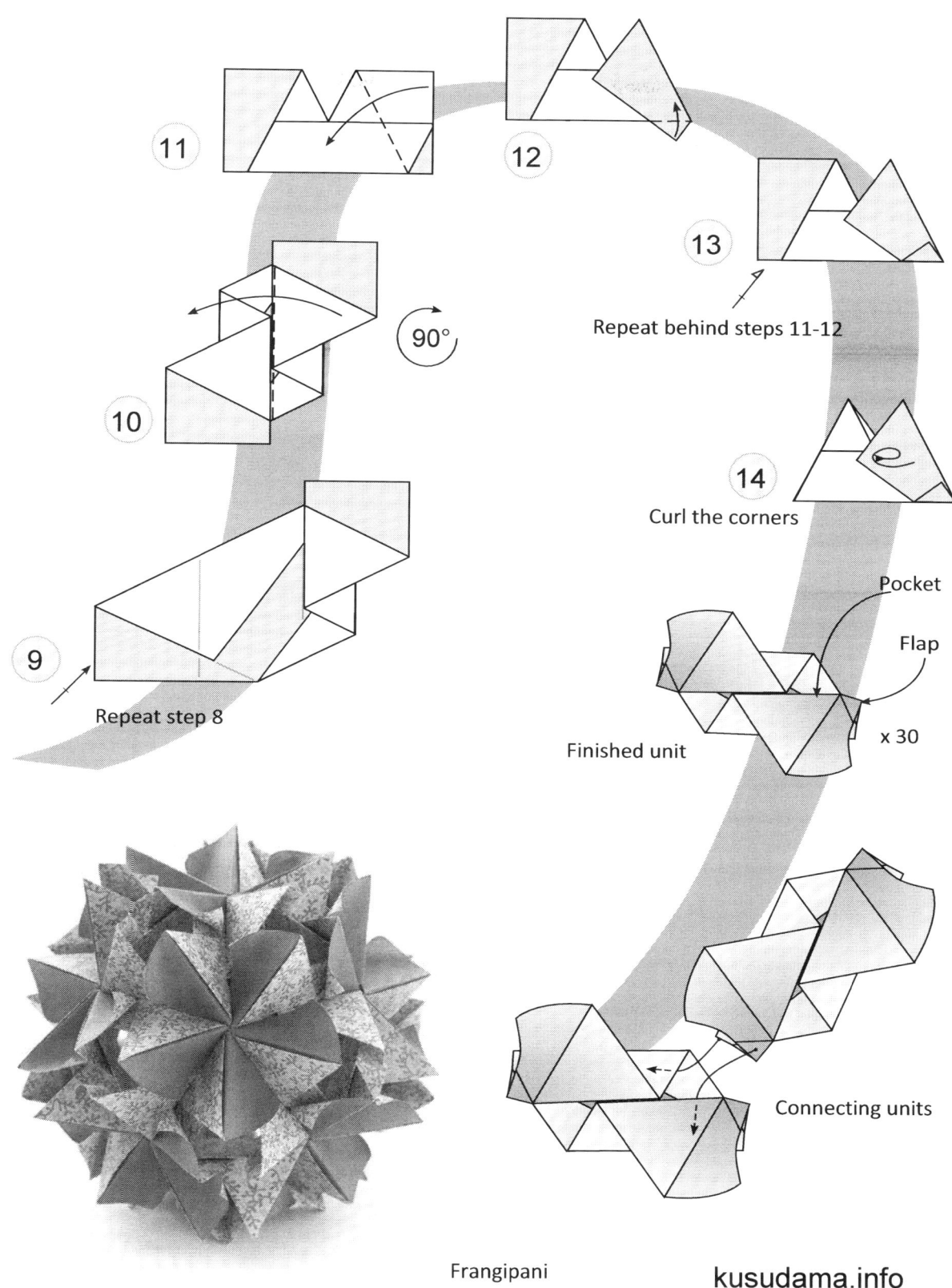

Frangipani

(Photo on back cover, second row, middle)

Cupidon

(Designed and diagrammed by Uniya Filonova, Russia, June 2014)

Paper: 7.5 x 7.5 cm, Units: 30, Final height: ~ 12 cm.

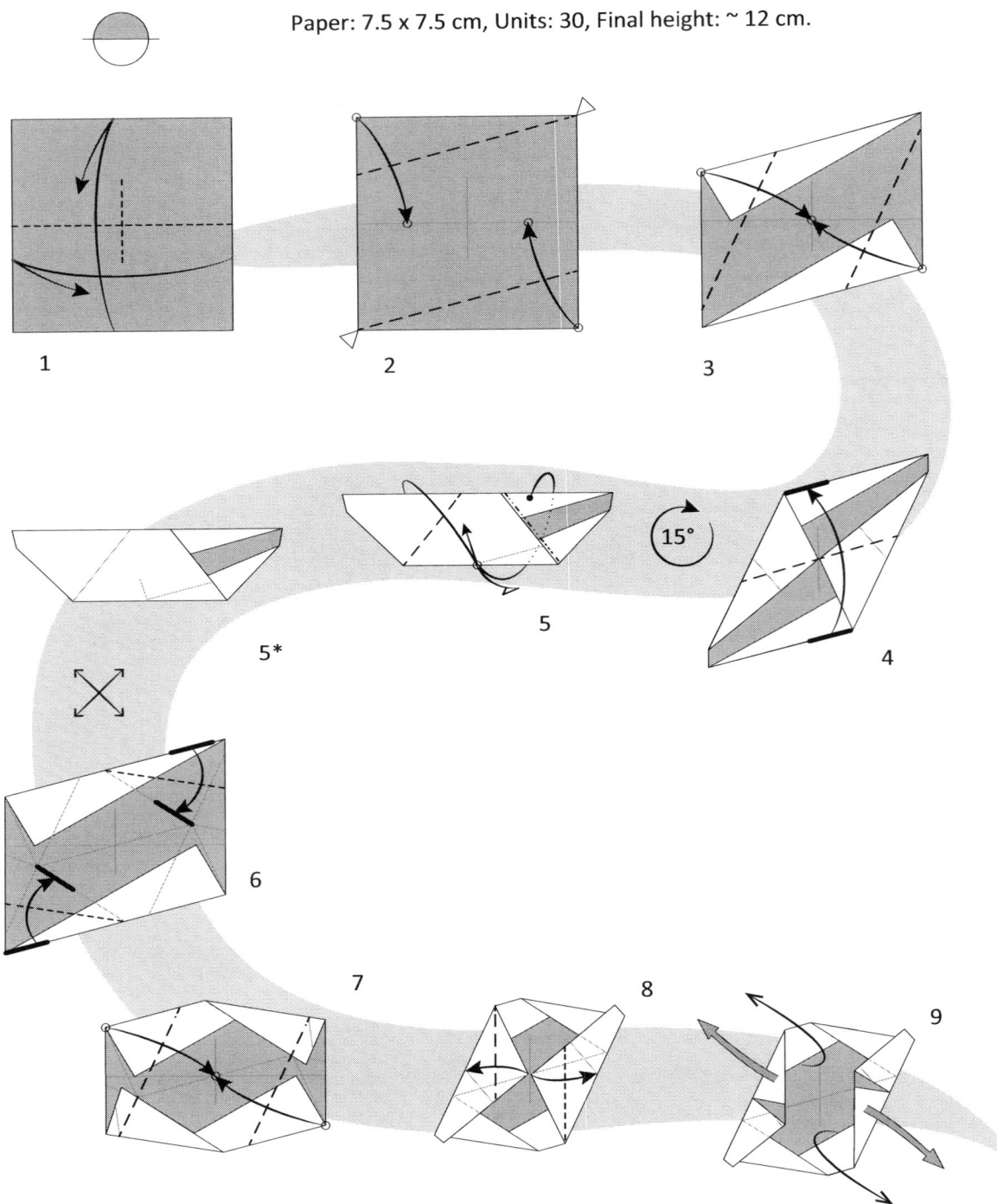

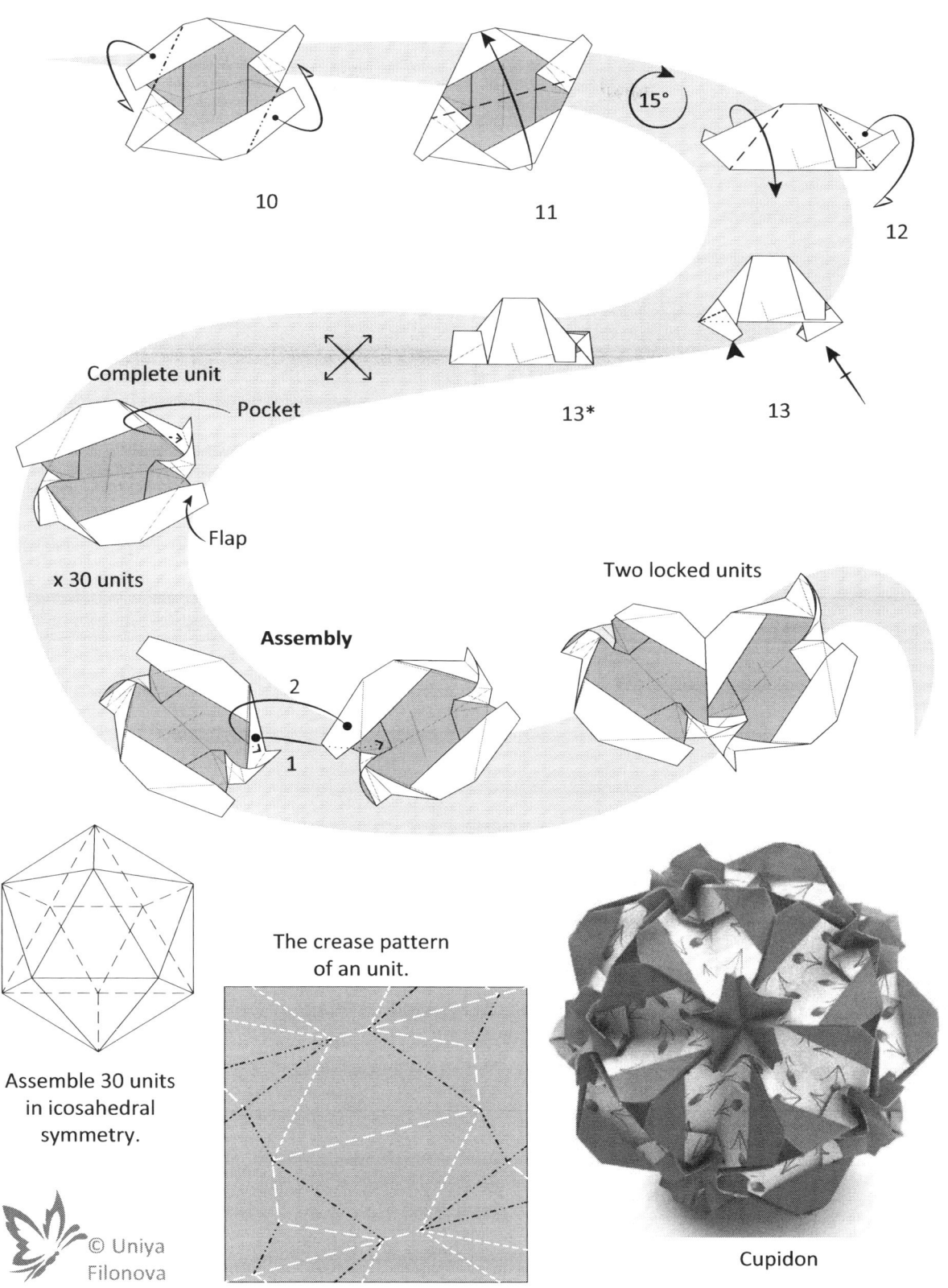

Cupidon

(Photo on back cover, second row, right)

Exquisite Modular Origami II

Crape Jasmine

(Designed and diagrammed by Narong Krined, Thailand, 2012)

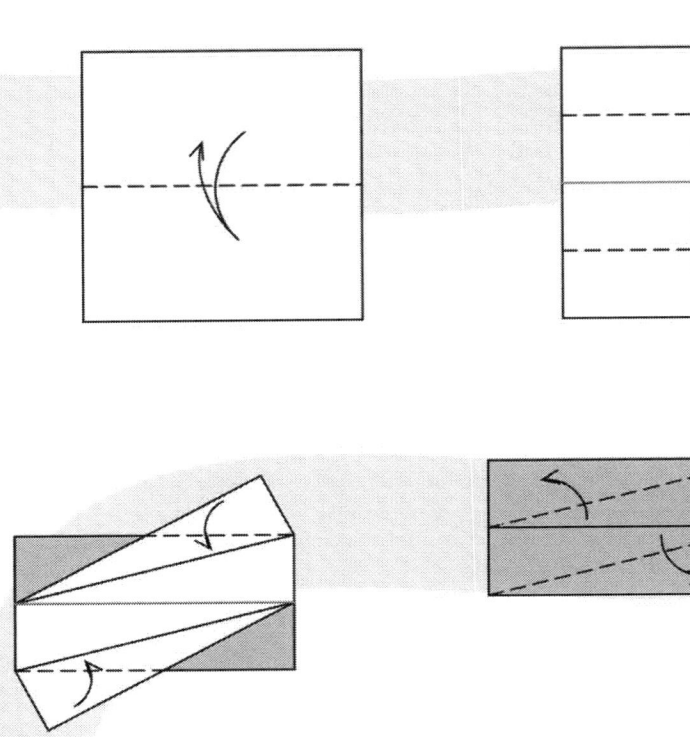

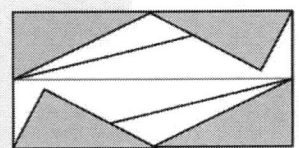

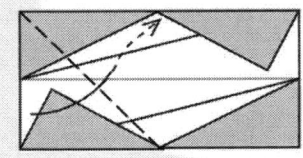

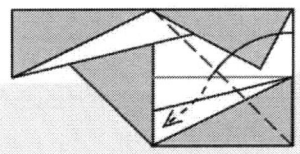

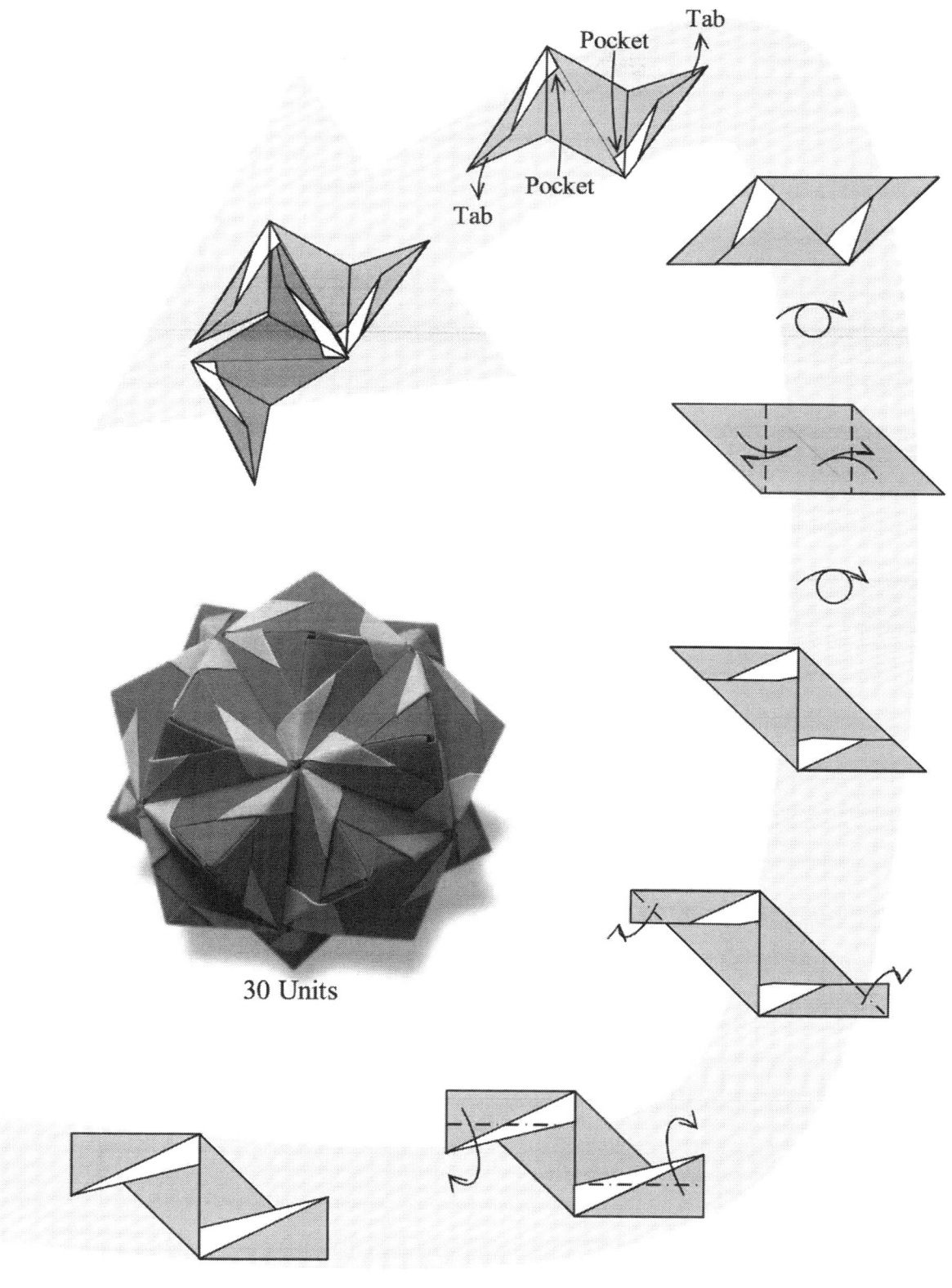

Assemble 30 units like a Sonobe model.

(Photo on back cover, second row, left)

Exquisite Modular Origami II

Bibliography and Suggested Reading

[Bee01] Rick Beech, *Origami: The Complete Practical Guide to the Ancient Art of Paperfolding,* Lorenz Books, 2001.

[Bri11] Marcela Brina, *Contemporary Origami Decorations: Beautiful Modular Origami Projects to Enlighten your Life*, CreateSpace, 2011.

[Bri13] Assia Brill, *Curlicue: Kinetic Origami*, CreateSpace 2013.

[Cox73] H. S. M. Coxeter, *Regular Polytopes*, Reprinted by Dover Publications, 1973.

[Dem07] Erik D. Demaine & Joseph O' Rourke, *Geometric Folding Algorithms, Linkages, Origami, Polyhedra*, Cambridge University Press, 2007.

[Dir97] Alexandra Dirk, *Origami Boxes for Gifts, Treasures and Trifles*, Sterling, 1997.

[Eng94] Peter Engel, *Origami from Angelfish to Zen*, Dover Publications, 1994.

[Eng11] Peter Engel, *Origami Odyssey: A Journey to the Edge of Paperfolding*, Tuttle Publishing, 2011.

[Fer07] Bruno Ferraz, *Ultrapassando Fronteiras com o Origami (Exceeding Borders with Origami)* (in Portugese), Editora Ciência Moderna, 2007.

[Fus89] Tomoko Fuse, *Origami Boxes*, Japan Publications Trading, 1989.

[Fus90] Tomoko Fuse, *Unit Origami: Multidimesional Transformations*, Japan Publications, 1990.

[Fus92] Tomoko Fuse, *Lets Fold Spirals,* Chikuma Shobo, 1992.

[Fus95] Tomoko Fuse, *Origami Spirals,* Chikuma Shobo, 1995.

[Fus96] Tomoko Fuse, *Joyful Origami Boxes*, Japan Publications Trading, 1996.

[Fus98] Tomoko Fuse, *Fabulous Origami Boxes*, Japan Publications Trading, 1998.

[Fus00] Tomoko Fuse, *Quick and Easy Origami Boxes*, Japan Publications Trading, 2000.

[Fus02] Tomoko Fuse, *Kusudama Origami*, Japan Publications Trading, 2002.

[Fus06] Tomoko Fuse, *Unit Polyhedron Origami,* Japan Publications Trading, 2006.

[Fus07] Tomoko Fuse, *Floral Origami Globes*, Japan Publications Trading, 2007.

[Fus10] Tomoko Fuse, *Unit Origami Essense*, Sun Trade Publishing, 2010.

[Fus10.1] Tomoko Fuse, *Unit Origami Fantasy*, Sun Trade Publishing, 2010.

[Fus12] Tomoko Fuse, *Spiral: Origami Art Design*, Verlag, 2012.

[Gil07] Eduardo Gil Moré, *Papiroflexia Y Geometría* (in Spanish), Miguel A Salvatella, 2007.

[Gje08] Eric Gjerde, *Origami Tessellations: Awe-Inspiring Geometric Designs*, A K Peters/CRC, 2008.

[Gro05] Gay Merrill Gross, Ornagami: An Origami Christmas at Your Fingertips, B&N, 2005.

[Gur95] Rona Gurkewitz and Bennett Arnstein, *3-D Geometric Origami: Modular Polyhedra*, Dover Publications, 1995.

[Gur99] Rona Gurkewitz, Bennett Arnstein, and Lewis Simon, *Modular Origami Polyhedra*, Dover Publications, 1999.

[Gur03] Rona Gurkewitz and Bennett Arnstein, *Multimodular Origami Polyhedra*, Dover Publications, 2003.

[Gur 08] Rona Gurkewitz, *Beginner's Book of Multimodular Origami Polyhedra: The Platonic Solids,* Dover Publications, 2008.

[Hul02] Thomas Hull, ed., *Origami 3: Third International Meeting of Origami Science, Mathematics, and Education,* A K Peters/CRC, 2002.

[Hul06] Thomas Hull, *Project Origami: Activities for Exploring Mathematics*, A K Peters/CRC, 2006.

[Jac87] Paul Jackson, *Encyclopedia of Origami/Papercraft Techniques*, Headline, 1987.

[Jac89] Paul Jackson, *Origami - A Complete Step-by-step Guide*, Hamlyn 1989.

[Kas98] Kunihiko Kasahara, *Origami for the Connoisseur*, Japan Publications, 1998.

[Kasa98] Kunihiko Kasahara, *Origami Omnibus: Paper Folding for Everybody*, Japan Publications, 1998.

[Kas03] Kunihiko Kasahara, *Extreme Origami*, Sterling, 2003.

[Kaw02] Miyuki Kawamura, *Polyhedron Origami for Beginners*, Japan Publications, 2002.

[Kawa01] Toshikazu Kawasaki, *Origami Dream World* (in Japanese), Asahipress, 2001.

[Kawa05] Toshikazu Kawasaki, *Roses, Origami & Math*, Japan Publications Trading, 2005.

[Kla09] Robert Klanten, *Papercraft: Design and Art With Paper*, Die Gestalten Verlag, 2009.

[Kot13] Flaviane Koti & Vera Young, *Origami em Flor: Kusudamas, Guirlandas e Buques*, CreateSpace, 2013.

[Kot15] Flaviane Koti & Vera Young, *O Origami e o Tempo: Flores, Borboletas, Kusudamas*, CreateSpace 2015.

[Lan03] Robert Lang, *Origami Design Secrets: Mathematical Methods for an Ancient Art*, A K Peters/CRC, 2003.

[Lan08] Robert Lang, ed., *Origami 4: Fourth International Meeting of Origami Science, Mathematics, and Education*, A K Peters/CRC, 2008.

[Lan11] Robert Lang, *Twists, Tilings, and Tessellations*, A K Peters/CRC Press, 2011.

[Lop16] Byriah Loper, *Mind-Blowing Modular Origami*, Tuttle Publishing, 2016.

[Luk14] Ekaterina Lukasheva, *Kusudama Origami Book*, Dover, 2014.

[Luk15] Ekaterina Lukasheva, *Modern Origami Kusudama*, CreateSpace 2015.

[Mit97] David Mitchell, *Mathematical Origami: Geometrical Shapes*, Tarquin, 1997.

[Mit00] David Mitchell, *Paper Crystals: How to Make Enchanting Ornaments*, Water Trade, 2000.

[Mon09] John Montroll, *Origami Polyhedra Design*, A K Peters/CRC, Ltd., 2009.

[Mon12] John Montroll, *Galaxy of Origami Stars*, CreateSpace, 2012.

[Mon14] John Montroll, *Origami Stars*, Dover, 2014.

[Muk07] Meenakshi Mukerji, *Marvelous Modular Origami*, A K Peters/CRC, 2007.

[Muk08] Meenakshi Mukerji, *Ornamental Origami: Exploring 3D Geometric Designs*, A K Peters/CRC, 2008.

[Muk10] Meenakshi Mukerji, *Origami Inspirations*, A K Peters/CRC, 2010.

[Muk11] Meenakshi Mukerji, *Exquisite Modular Origami*, CreateSpace, 2011.

[Muk13] Meenakshi Mukerji, *Wondrous One Sheet Origami*, CreateSpace, 2013.

[NOA94] NOA, *Minna Kusudama*, Nihon Origami Kyokai, 1994.

[Nol13] J. C. Nolan, Creating Origami, 2013.

[Ow96] Francis Ow, *Origami Hearts*, Japan Publications, 1996.

[Pet 98] David Petty, *Origami Wreaths and Rings*, Aitoh, 1998.

[Pet02] David Petty, *Origami 1-2-3*, Sterling, 2002.

[Pet06] David Petty, *Origami A-B-C*, Sterling, 2006.

[Rom15] Natalia Romanenko, *Kusudama - Magic paper Balls*, Airis Press, 2015.

[Rob04] Nick Robinson, *The Encyclopedia Of Origami*, Running Press, 2004.

[Row66] Tandalam Sundara Row, *Geometric Exercises in Paper Folding*, Reprinted by Dover Publications, 1966.

[Tan02] Origami Tanteidan, *Origami Tanteidan Convention No.8,* Origami House, 2002.

[Tem 86] Florence Temko, *Paper Pandas and Jumping Frogs,* China Books & Periodicals, 1986.

[Tem04] Florence Temko, *Origami Boxes and More*, Tuttle Publishing, 2004.

[Tub 06] Arnold Tubis and Crystal Mills, *Unfolding Mathematics with Origami Boxes*, Key Curriculum Press, 2006.

[Tub07] Arnold Tubis and Crystal Mills, *Fun with Folded Fabric Boxes*, C&T Publishing 2007.

[Wan11] Patsy Wang-Iverson, Robert Lang, Mark Yim, *Origami 5: Fifth International Meeting of Origami Science, Mathematics, and Education*, A K Peters/CRC, 2011.

[Yam90] Makoto Yamaguchi, *Kusudama Ball Origami*, Japan Publications, 1990.

Suggested Websites

Sara Adams, *Happy Folding*, http://www.happyfolding.com/

Gilad Aharoni, *Gilad's Origami Page*, http://www.giladorigami.com/

Krystyna & Wojtek Burczyk, *Burczyk Origami*, http://www1.zetosa.com.pl/~burczyk/origami/

George Hart, *The Pavilion of Polyhedreality*, http://www.georgehart.com/pavilion.html

Tom Hull, *Origami Mathematics Page*, http://mars.wne.edu/~thull/origamimath.html

Rachel Katz, *Origami with Rachel Katz*, http://www.origamiwithrachelkatz.com

Michał Kosmulski, Modular Origami, http://michal.kosmulski.org/origami/

Robert Lang, *Robert J. Lang Origami*, http://www.langorigami.com/

Ekaterina Lukasheva, *Kusudama me!*, http://kusudama.me/

David Mitchell, *Origami Heaven*, http://www.origamiheaven.com/

Meenakshi Mukerji, *Origami By Meenakshi*, http://www.origamee.net/, facebook.com/origamee.net

Francis Ow, *Francis Ow's Origami Page*, http://www.nickrobinson.info/clients/owrigami/

David Petty, *Dave's Origami Emporium*, http://www.davidpetty.me.uk/

Jim Plank, *Jim Plank's Origami Page*, http://www.cs.utk.edu/~plank/plank/origami/

Nick Robinson, *professional origami artist and author*, http://www.nickrobinson.info/origami/

Natalia Romanenko, *Kusudama*, http://kusudama.info/

Halina Rosciszewska-Narloch, *Haligami World*, http://www.origami.friko.pl

Yuri & Katrin Shumakov, *Oriland*, http://www.oriland.com

Maria Sinayskaya, *Go Origami! Kusudama and Modular Origami,* http://goorigami.com/

Nicolas Terry, Passion Origami, http://www.passion-origami.com/

Leyla Torres, *Origami Spirit*, http://www.origamispirit.com/

Paula Versnick, *Orihouse*, http://www.orihouse.com/

Dennis Walker, *Dennis Walker's Origami Page*, http://www.prospero78.freeserve.co.uk/

Dennis Walker, *Origami Database,* http://origamidatabase.com/

Joseph Wu, *Joseph Wu Origami,* http://www.origami.vancouver.bc.ca/

Evan Zodl, *EZ Origami I Origami For Everyone*, http://ez-origami.com/

British Origami Society, *BOS Home Page*, http://britishorigami.info/

Japan Origami Academic Society, *Origami Tanteidan*, http://www.origami.gr.jp/index-e.html

OrigamiUSA, *Welcome to OrigamiUSA!*, http://origamiusa.org/

Origami Resource Center, *Origami: the Art of Paper Folding*, http://www.origami-resource-center.com/index.html

About Author and Guest Contributors

Meenakshi Mukerji (Adhikari) was introduced to origami in early childhood by her uncle Bireshwar Mukhopadhyay. She rediscovered origami in its modular form as an adult quite by chance in 1995, when a friend, Shobha Prabakar, took her to a modular origami class taught by Doug Philips. This newfound mathematical and structural side of modular origami rekindled her passion for the art, and soon after, she started designing and displaying origami on her popular website origamee.net. The website features colorful photo galleries and links to a myriad of free diagrams, with over a million and a half hits to date.

In 2005, OrigamiUSA presented her with the Florence Temko award for generously sharing her work on her website. In April 2007, her first book *Marvelous Modular Origami* was published followed in quick succession by four more books, listed on the next page. She has been a featured artist and a special guest at many origami conventions both in the USA and abroad. Although known for modular designs, she has published a book of her single sheet works, which has also been well received.

Meenakshi regularly contributes to various origami journals and exhibits her work at conventions. She is a member of OrigamiUSA and British Origami Society, and an editor for OrigamiUSA's online magazine *The Fold*. People who have provided her with much origami encouragement and inspiration are the late David Petty, Rosalinda Sanchez, Robert Lang, Francis Ow, Rona Gurkewitz, Ravi Apte, Rachel Katz, and the numerous visitors of her website.

Born and raised in Kolkata, India, Meenakshi obtained her BS in electrical engineering from the Indian Institute of Technology, Kharagpur, and a MS in computer science from Portland State University, Oregon. She then worked as a software engineer for more than a decade. She is now at home in California devoting her time to family, designing and authoring origami and, of course, spreading the joy of origami.

Author's Website

Origami by Meenakshi (http://www.origamee.net): Maintained by the author since 1997 until present, colorful and vibrant, the website features photo galleries of her own works as well as others' works folded by her. Additionally you will find a large collection of free diagrams of some of her designs and links to those of other people's designs. It has been one of the top websites for "modular origami" worldwide web search and has had over a million and a half hits. As is evident from the visitor guestbook comments, the site is a wonderful resource for origami lovers. Some have noted that they have found folding from the site to be therapeutic and relaxing. The site has enticed modular origami skeptics as well. Please also visit facebook.com/origamee.net.

Author's Other Books

Marvelous Modular Origami,
AKPeters/CRC, Apr 2007.
ISBN: 978-1568813165

Ornamental Origami,
AKPeters/CRC, Dec 2008.
ISBN: 978-1568814452

Origami Inspirations,
AKPeters/CRC Aug 2010.
ISBN: 978-1568815848

Exquisite Modular Origami,
CreateSpace, Nov 2011.
ISBN: 978-1463707606

Wondrous One Sheet Origami,
CreateSpace, Dec 2013.
ISBN: 978-1463707606

Some Praises:

"Meenakshi Mukerji's work is both intricate and lovely. She's greatly respected in the origami world, one of the well-known world leaders in modular origami. Her books offer a nice exposition of the mathematical elements, but you're not being hit over the head with math lessons. You learn things without even realizing that you have."

— Dr. Robert Lang, world renowned origami artist and author.
(In an interview in The San Jose Mercury News, 2008).

"Meenakshi Mukerji is one of today's masters of modular origami, designs comprised of multiple pieces of paper. She also brings her ingenuity and creativity to designs made from a single piece of paper. Among the most appealing aspects of her single sheet work is the way she subtly manipulates a purely geometric form to fold a flower, a leaf, a butterfly, or card suits."
— Peter Engel, author of *Origami from Angelfish to Zen* and other books.
(In Foreword for *Wondrous One Sheet origami,* 2013).

"Meenakshi's models are paper folding in its purest form. They range from simple Sonobe to floral and geometric constructions. All are eye-catching and satisfying to fold, and the finished constructions are pleasing to behold."
— David Petty, author *of Origami A-B-C* and other books.
(On back cover of *Marvelous Modular Origami,* 2007).

Natalia Romanenko

Natalia Romanenko of Moldova is a prolific modular origami designer. She is a computer programmer by profession and worked in the banking sector for a while, but after having her first child she decided to leave her dream job. While her son was growing up, she folded paper boats, planes and simple animals for playing games with him. Towards the end of 2010, she searched the Internet for some Christmas crafts to make with her son. She became interested in the Chinese Venture Units and that is when her modular origami journey began.

Soon afterwards she found polyhedral modular origami which impressed her so much that once she began folding, she couldn't stop. Her favorite subject at school was Mathematics (Algebra and Geometry), and she always liked to solve difficult problems. She thinks probably that is why modular origami has become her passion. She started out by reverse engineering the models she saw on the Internet and liked and that eventually led to creating her own designs. She also likes folding complex origami figures from a single sheet of paper.

Natalia has published her designs in various origami journals and just released a new book *Kusudama - Magic Paper Balls* (978-5811252480). She is delighted to be invited to contribute to this book for which she chose her beautiful Frangipani design from March 2013. She maintains a beautiful website, kusudama.info, which has tons of free folding instructions. She also has a stunning Flickr® gallery,flickr.com/photos/ronatka/. She makes use of a vast range of lovely papers to fold her models and pays great attention to precise folding. Her photography is quite impressive as well.

Uniya Filonova

Uniya Filonova of Russia has a background in Chemical Pharmaceuticals and has been folding modular origami for only a few years. Almost immediately after she folded her first *kusudama*, she started creating her own modulars, of which there is a surprisingly large number for the short period of time that she has been designing. Her design process involves, in her own words, "first molding the paper like clay in her mind, and then thinking through the geometry and corresponding steps."

Uniya generously shares photos and free instructions of her designs in her blog stranamasterov.ru/user/122381. She also maintains a beautiful Flickr® Gallery flickr.com/photos/79348234@N06/ where she shares photos of her own designs as well as other people's designs.

Narong Krined

Narong Krined is an Assistant Professor of mathematics at Phetchaburi Rajabhat University in Thailand. He is also an origami enthusiast and has quite a few Sonobe designs of his own. Narong started folding about 10 years ago mainly from books he purchased in Japan and from the tons of origami material available on the Internet. He likes all kinds of origami, modulars being his passion. He published a book titled *Sonobe Variations* (ISBN 978-6167330129) in 2012 and as the name implies, the book consists entirely of Sonobe unit variations with color change patterns.

You can follow Narong's vibrantly colorful work on OrigamiMathThailand page: facebook.com/OrigamiMathThailand

The designs in this book are pure origami requiring no cuts or glue. If necessary, cutting is employed for the initial sizing of the paper only, and not thereafter.

Printed in Great Britain
by Amazon